THE Process Reengineering WORKBOOK

Practical Steps
to Working
Faster and Smarter
Through
Process Improvement

THE Process Reengineering WORKBOOK

Practical Steps
to Working
Faster and Smarter
Through
Process Improvement

Jerry L. Harbour

QUALITY RESOURCES ®
A Division of The Kraus Organization Limited

902 Broadway, New York, New York 10010

Most Quality Resources books are available at quantity discounts when purchased in bulk. For more information contact:

Special Sales Department
Quality Resources
A Division of The Kraus Organization Limited
902 Broadway
New York, New York 10010
800-247-8519

Copyright © 1994 Jerry L. Harbour

All rights reserved. No part of this work covered by the copyrights hereon may be reproduced or used in any form or by any means—graphic, electronic, or mechanical, including photocopying, recording, taping, or information storage and retrieval systems—without written permission of the publisher.

Printed in the United States of America

97 96 95   10 9 8 7 6 5 4 3 2

Quality Resources
A Division of The Kraus Organization Limited
902 Broadway
New York, New York 10010
800-247-8519

The paper used in this publication meets the minimum requirements of American National Standard for Information Sciences—Permanence of Paper for Printed Library Materials, ANSI Z39.48-1984.

ISBN 0-527-76240-7

Library of Congress Cataloging-in-Publication Data

Harbour, Jerry L.
    The process reengineering workbook : practical steps to working faster and smarter through process improvement / Jerry L. Harbour.
      p.   cm.
    Includes bibliographical references (p.   ) and index.
    ISBN 0-527-76240-7
    1. Organizational change.   2. Organizational effectiveness.
3. Time management.   4. Industrial organization.   I. Title.
HD58.8.H3638   1994
  650.1—dc20
                                            94-14109
                                              CIP

Dedicated to
Megan and **Chris**
my children

Table of Contents

Preface ix
Acknowledgments xi

ONE: **Better, Faster, and Cheaper** 1
TWO: **Work and Waste** 6
THREE: **Work Processes** 17
FOUR: **Process Analysis and Measurement** 36
FIVE: **The Seven-Step PI Method** 55
SIX: **Process Improvement Principles** 85
SEVEN: **Case Studies** 103
EIGHT: **Some Final Comments** 116

Glossary 127
Exercise Solutions 130
Suggested Reading 138
Index 141

Preface

"It's not all that complicated. Our mission is to do everything better, faster, and cheaper than our competition. If we can't do that, we'll be out of business before we know it. Then we won't have a mission."

I remember hearing those words a number of years ago. They were voiced by a concerned CEO of a large international corporation. They are as true today as they were then. In fact, they're even more relevant in today's highly competitive marketplace.

At the time I heard those comments, I was immersed in the quality movement of the early 1980s. I was participating in quality circles, reading all of the right books, learning statistical process control (SPC) and the other quality tools, speaking the language, and spreading the total quality management (TQM) gospel.

So I certainly believed the *better* part. I could even understand the *cheaper* part. But did we really need to do things *faster* as well? Wasn't that asking a bit much?

Much has changed since I first heard those comments some ten years ago. Some companies have become better. They have successfully launched quality programs, and they have reaped the benefits of those efforts.

However, in today's business world, doing things better is no longer enough. It's certainly important, but it's not enough. We're entering a new era. An era in which customer satisfaction and business success depend as much on *speed* as they do on the cost and quality of the goods we produce and the services we provide. Doing things faster has become just as important as doing them better and cheaper. *Better, Faster*, and *Cheaper*. We may not like it, but it is the new reality of the 90s.

The question, then, is how do we become better, faster, and cheaper? Many suggest the answer is *process reengineering*—the new buzzwords of the 90s. Sounds great. I like it. But how do we do process reengineering? How do we roll up our sleeves, get down in the trenches, and actually reengineer our core work processes? How do we eliminate process waste? Waste that adds only unnecessary delay and business costs—things companies can ill afford.

I began searching for some answers. I wanted to find some techniques that could make reengineering possible. I read books. New books and some great, old ones. I studied—the U.S., the Japanese, anyone and everyone. I talked to people. I observed different processes from various industries—energy, manufacturing, mining, transportation. I tried out some of my ideas and techniques. I taught courses. I gave lectures. I launched process improvement teams. Some worked. Some didn't. I kept refining. Going back to the drawing board. Rethinking. The results? This book, *The Process Reengineering Workbook*.

The Process Reengineering Workbook is for those of us who are charged with doing it. Not just talking about it or philosophizing about it, but actually making it happen. It's a book of applied techniques, tools, and tips. In short, it's a hands-on book about eliminating waste from the workplace.

The Process Reengineering Workbook is geared to today's diverse business and industry mix—manufacturing, service, transportation, knowledge, etc. It's as relevant to companies processing information and producing paper as it is to more traditional manufacturing operations. Indeed, many of the generic examples and case studies used throughout the book are from non-manufacturing settings.

I hope, you'll find *The Process Reengineering Workbook* easy to use and understand. More important, I hope the book makes your job easier, safer, less frustrating, and more enjoyable, and your company more competitive.

Acknowledgments

The writing of a book is never an individual effort. There are so many people to thank, acknowledge, and pay tribute to. *The Process Reengineering Workbook* is no exception.

Before thanking and acknowledging those special people, however, I'd like to pay tribute to a process reengineer extraordinaire: Frank Gilbreth (1868–1924). Many of Gilbreth's concepts and techniques are as applicable in today's high-tech information age as they were 100 years ago. His ideas—eliminating waste, doing things faster, and using technology to improve processes—form the basis of this book.

I'd like to gratefully acknowledge my colleagues and work associates, especially Dr. Allan Johnson and Carol Somers. I'd also like to acknowledge and warmly thank those who have survived my many training and consulting endeavors, and who have freely and graciously shared with me their real-world experiences, ideas, and insights on process improvement. In addition, I'd like to thank my editor, Cynthia Tokumitsu of Quality Resouces. Ms. Tokumitsu's professionalism, creativity, and friendliness have made her a delight to work with. Finally, I'd like to thank and warmly acknowledge Dr. Elda Zounar, my wife. Her emotional support and constant encouragement during this effort have been invaluable. Thank you to all.

Jerry L. Harbour, Ph.D.

ONE

Better, Faster, and Cheaper

Massive Layoffs Announced
Year-end Profits Plummet
Foreign Competition Threatens Domestic Industry
Company Files Bankruptcy

Every day we read such headlines. Companies are laying off people. Companies are losing money. Companies are threatened by foreign competitors. Companies are seeking legal protection. In short, companies are experiencing lots of problems.

What's the cause of all of these problems? It depends on who you talk to. Workers believe it's incompetent managers. Managers believe it's lazy workers. Corporate CEOs blame it on everything: incompetent managers, lazy workers, a sluggish economy, unfair trade practices, increased global competition, a growing national debt, and so on.

What's interesting in all of this finger pointing is that we seem to desperately want someone to blame. A *who* if you will. A who that represents a worker, a manager, or a foreign competitor. Instead of wasting all of this energy searching for a scapegoat, a who to blame, perhaps we should change our focus from the *who* to the *what*. What's a what you ask? A what represents the various work *processes* that we are all a part of. A what is how we do our jobs. A what is what we do to produce a product, complete a task, or provide a service.

> **pro•cess:** the blending and transformation of a specific set of inputs into a set of outputs. A process is what we do in order to produce a product, complete a task, or render a service.

The *Process Reengineering Workbook* is all about fixing the what, not the who. It's about doing work better, faster, and cheaper than our competition—

whether that competition is just across the street, across an adjoining border, or across a vast and empty ocean. But the *Process Reengineering Workbook* is not just about doing everything better, faster, and cheaper. It's about making our core business processes—the things that really count—better, faster, and cheaper.

> **re•en•gi•neer•ing:** the radical redesign of a particular process to achieve dramatic improvements in speed, cost, quality, and service. Akin to throwing the baby out with the bathwater and starting over from scratch.

You might ask why we have to do things better, faster, and cheaper? Who really cares? Try to remember the last time someone brought you a work assignment and said, "Here's something I want you to do. Take as long as you want and spend as much money as you wish. And I don't care how well it's done either!" It sounds great doesn't it? Unfortunately, this type of job assignment rarely, if ever happens. Instead, most of us get tasks that demand high quality and low cost. And of course, they must be completed yesterday.

We're finding that today's business world is changing. Customer satisfaction and business success increasingly depend on the speed, cost, and quality of the goods we produce and the services we provide. The new buzzwords of the 1990s are innovation, speed, flexibility, adaptability, service, and quality. If our companies are to compete and thrive in this new environment, we must make significant changes. We have to begin to rethink and reengineer how we do business. We need to reengineer the *what*—our work processes—to learn how to work smarter, not harder.

About This Book

The *Process Reengineering Workbook* is all about fixing the *what*. It's about improving and reengineering our work processes, and making those processes better, faster, and cheaper. It's also about making work simpler, easier, safer, less frustrating, and hopefully, more enjoyable and rewarding for all of us.

The book is based on a few simple principles:

- Focus on the what—the work process—not the who.
- Use the who to fix the what.
- Eliminate process waste.
- Simplify everything.
- Combine various process steps.
- Design processes with alternative process pathways.

- Whenever possible let the customer assist in the process.
- Use technology to significantly improve process performance.

When combined with some simple tools and techniques, these few principles can dramatically improve our work processes. They can:

- Increase output quality.
- Decrease process costs.
- Compress process cycle times (a measurement of process speed).

How will we go about learning all of these good things? By simply taking them one step at a time.

Chapter 2 is called "Work and Waste." It divides the time we spend on the job into two components: work and waste. *Work* represents all value-adding process activities. Work moves a process forward. *Waste* represents all non-value adding process activities. Process waste adds only delay and cost—things that companies can ill afford. To significantly improve our work processes, we must:

- Understand the difference between work and waste.
- Identify all activities that represent waste.
- Eliminate or minimize all process waste.

Chapter 2 provides many examples of work and waste. Some you'll recognize. Others you may find surprising.

Chapter 3 is titled "Work Processes." A work process is the blending and transformation of a set of inputs into a specific set of outputs. *Inputs* can include people, materials, energy, equipment, and procedures. An *output* can be a product, a service, or the completion of a specific task. A process typically contains six basic process steps:

1. Operation.
2. Inspection.
3. Transportation.
4. Delay.
5. Storage.
6. Rework.

Some of these process steps are work or value-adding activities—good things. Most others, however, are waste or non-value adding process activities—bad things that add only process delay and cost. Chapter 3 contains examples of each type of process step. It also provides an opportunity to practice identifying the various types of process steps.

Chapter 4 is called "Process Analysis and Measurement." To improve a process, we must first learn something about it. That something is captured by conducting a process analysis. A process analysis is a description of the different types of steps associated with a particular process. It identifies both value-adding (i.e., work) and non-value adding (i.e., waste) process steps. The goal of a process analysis is to significantly improve the process. Various types of process-related measurements—called metrics—are also described in Chapter 4. Time and cost are two examples of process metrics. Chapter 4 includes examples of the techniques and tools used in process analysis. It also provides an opportunity to practice using them.

Chapter 5 is called "The Seven-Step PI Method." The chapter presents a simple seven-step method for analyzing and improving work processes. This is the how-to-do-it chapter. The seven-step method involves:

1. Defining process boundaries.
2. Observing process flow.
3. Collecting process-related data.
4. Analyzing collected data.
5. Targeting improvement areas.
6. Developing improvements.
7. Implementing and monitoring improvements.

The method is easy to use and follow. It provides the key ingredients to successful process reengineering. These ingredients include:

- Collecting needed process data quickly and at the right level.
- Analyzing it.
- Identifying the weak spots and needed improvement areas.
- Selecting and implementing an appropriate improvement strategy as quickly as possible.

Chapter 5 also presents two case studies. The case studies demonstrate how easy it is to use the seven-step PI method.

Chapter 6 is titled "Process Improvement Tips." It offers practical ideas, in the form of nine basic principles, for improving processes. Each principle is illustrated with examples that show how it works. Chapter 6 covers many issues, including using technology more effectively. After Chapter 6, the world of high tech may never be quite the same!

Chapter 7, "Case Studies," lets you apply what you've learned. The chapter presents five case studies from various industry and business settings. The goal of each case study is to make the process better, faster, cheaper, or safer. Chapter 7 lets you practice and apply everything you've learned about process reengineering.

Chapter 8 is titled "Some Final Comments." It summarizes all of the important points you have learned. It also offers some final thoughts about process reengineering and dispels some commonly held myths.

Each chapter is full of practical examples, useful hints, and hands-on exercises. The intent of *The Process Reengineering Workbook* is not to provide a textbook on process reengineering. Rather, the goal is to provide a useful set of techniques and tools: a toolbox that will let you make a difference in the workplace almost immediately.

The ideas, techniques, and tools presented in *The Process Reengineering Workbook* apply to any work setting. Whether you process insurance claims in a large office complex, manufacture automobile parts in a factory, ship materials cross country, care for patients in a hospital, mine gold in the mountainous highlands of New Guinea, or perform a myriad of other work activities, you are part of a work process. And all work processes share basic, fundamental characteristics that can be significantly improved and reengineered.

No matter what industry or company you represent, everyone wants the same thing: Improve quality, do things faster, decrease costs. Better, Faster, and Cheaper. We may not like it, but for better or worse, it is the new reality of the 90s. The good news is that companies are drastically improving the way they do business. They are becoming more competitive. They are improving quality, compressing cycle times, and slashing process costs. The key to this success? Letting the *who*—represented by folks just like you—fix the *what*.

Enjoy.

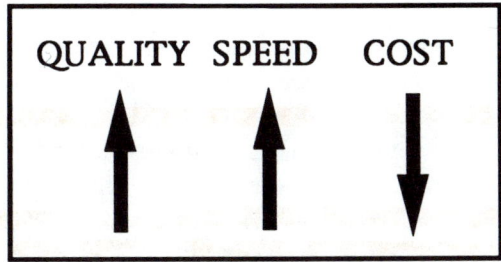

TWO

Work and Waste

Fill in the blank: We are paid for our _____.

Most of us probably scribbled in the word "work." After all, we're hired to work and it's only logical that we get paid for our work. But is this really true? Although we're certainly hired to work, most of us are actually paid for our time. We receive so much money per hour, month, or year. We punch a time clock, not a work clock. We fill out a weekly time card, not a weekly work card. Indeed, most of us are paid for our time, not our work.

The time we spend on the job can be divided into two components: work and waste (see Figure 2.1). This work/waste concept is important. The goal of process reengineering is eliminating all process-related waste.

What do we mean by the terms work and waste? If we look work up in a dictionary, we find that it refers to:

Physical or mental effort or activity directed toward the production or accomplishment of something.

It means "to labor." On the basis of this definition, greater productivity can result only from greater mental or physical effort—that is, working harder but not necessarily working smarter.

In process reengineering, the word work has a much different meaning. We will use the term work only when a certain activity is moving a process forward or directly adding value. Remember, a process is the blending and transformation of a set of specific inputs into a particular output. Outputs can include:

- A product.
- The completion of a task.
- A service.

Work occurs whenever an activity is moving a process forward or adding value to an output (see Table 2.1).

6

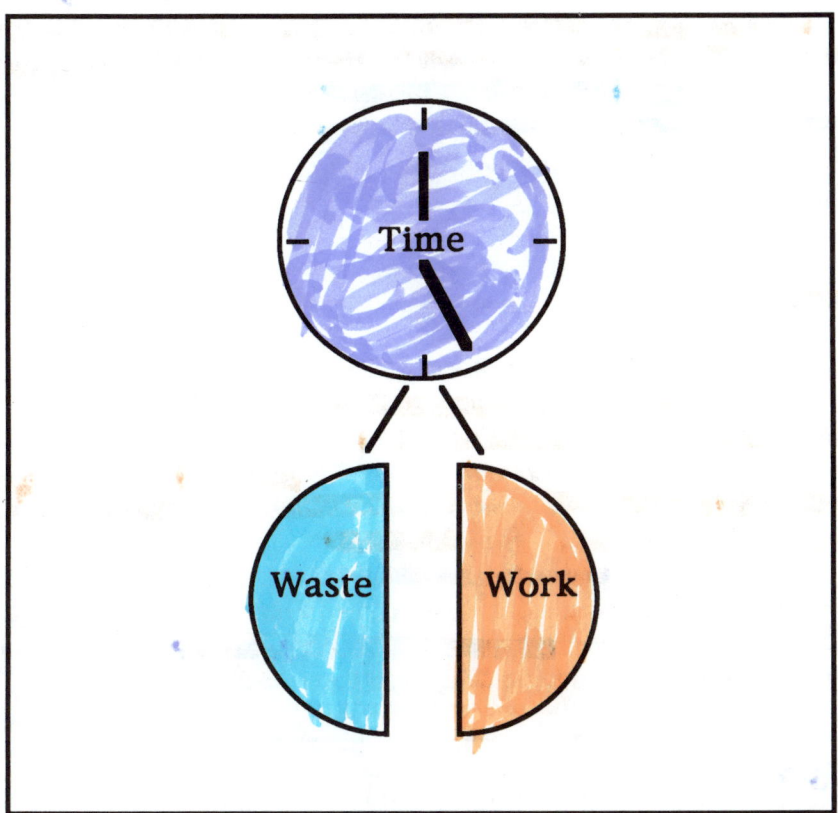

Figure 2.1

To understand what we mean by the phrase "adding value" to an output, think of a widget assembly process. The assembled widget is an output. An assembled widget comes complete with body, legs, arms, and head. When we're placing the legs, arms, and head on the body, we're adding value to the widget output. People pay money for an assembled widget. However, if we have to stand around waiting to get widget arm or leg parts, that's not adding value to the output. That waiting time is a delay. It's not adding value because it's not moving the assemble-widget process forward.

WORK	WASTE
• Adds value	• Adds delay
• Moves process forward	• Adds cost

Table 2.1

8 | *The Process Reengineering Workbook*

Waste then represents all non-value adding process activities. Waste includes wasted effort, time, materials, motion, and costs. Waste does not enhance value or move a process forward. Instead, waste adds only delay and cost.

Work is good. We want to maximize it. However, waste, is bad. We always want to eliminate it or at least minimize it. Let's look at some examples of work and waste on the following pages to better understand these two important concepts.

Example 1

After picking up a number of groceries at the supermarket, you go to the checkout stand to begin the checking-out process. During the checkout process, the grocery clerk passes each item over a scanner. You notice that the scan is usually successful and the price registers on the display. Sometimes, however, the scan is unsuccessful. When this happens, the clerk often has to repeat the scan several times before the price is successfully recorded.

In this example, a successful scan is work. It is moving the checking-out process forward. That is, it's getting you, the customer, out of the store in an efficient manner. However, an unsuccessful scan, is waste. Instead of moving the process forward, it is adding delay (see Figure 2.2).

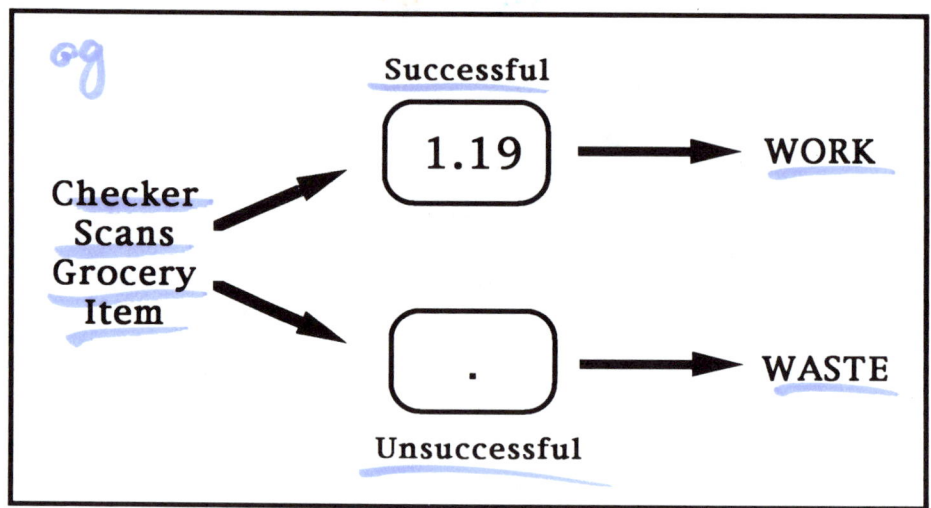

Figure 2.2

Key Point

Work and waste typically require the same amount of physical effort. In the grocery store example, an unsuccessful scan requires the same amount of physical exertion as a successful scan. Waste also costs a company the same amount of money as work. For example, the same wage is paid for an unsuccessful scan as for a successful scan. Companies lose lots of money paying for waste.

Example 2

Working as a field engineer, you maintain and repair complex hospital imaging and X-ray equipment. To perform your job, you must frequently refer to a number of bulky field manuals and lengthy procedures. These reference materials, which weigh about 150 pounds, are stored on a shelf in your service van. During a typical service call, you make several trips to your van to look up information. In fact, approximately 15 percent of your time is spent walking back and forth to your van.

In this example, 15 percent of your time is waste. Time spent walking back and forth to the van searching for information only delays the maintenance-and-repair process. Such delay is waste. Using the information you retrieve is a value-adding activity. Retrieving it is a non-value adding activity. Whether it takes you 10 minutes or 15 minutes to retrieve the information, the value of the information is still the same (see Figure 2.3).

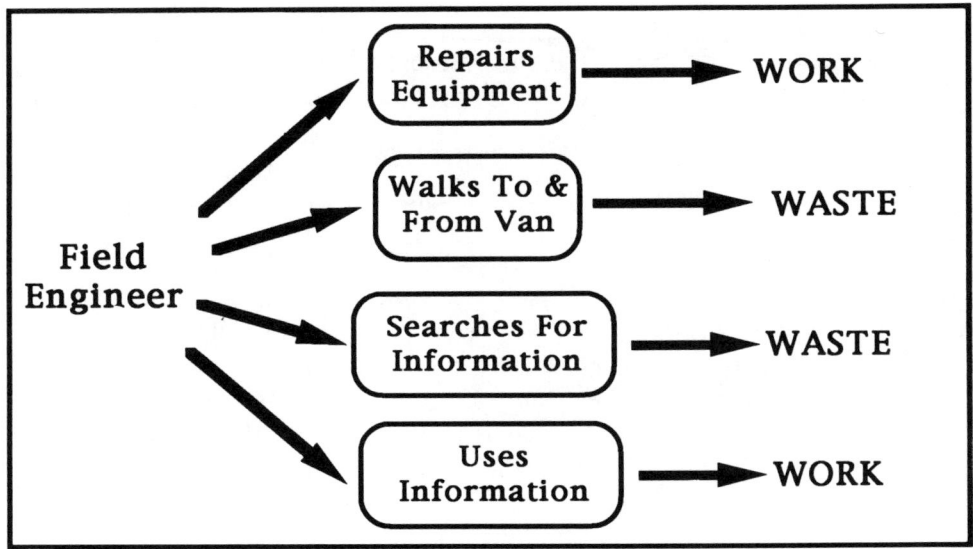

Figure 2.3

Key Point   To determine whether an activity is work or waste, ask yourself: If this activity is eliminated, will the quality of the output be affected? For example, if the field engineer retrieves the information in another way, does the quality of the output—maintaining and repairing the imaging equipment— suffer? In this case, the answer is no. Walking back and forth does not add value to the service process. Instead, it adds only delay, which is waste.

Example 3

Working at a large factory, you receive a part that fails a quality inspection because it was assembled incorrectly. You spend approximately two hours breaking down the part and assembling it correctly.

In this example, the two hours spent repairing the defective part is waste (see Figure 2.4). This type of waste is called *rework*. Rework does not move the assembly process forward. Instead, it is a process delay. Rework is a common form of waste. Ideally, processes should never include any rework.

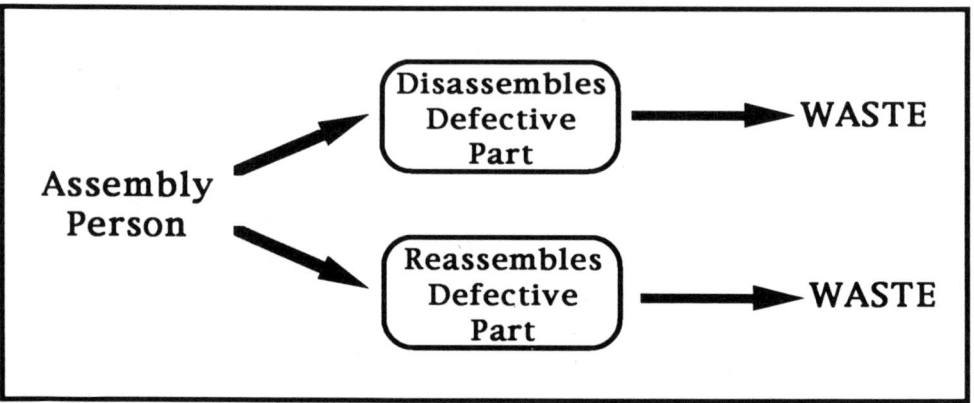

Figure 2.4

Key Point

Rework is a fairly obvious example of waste, but what about the quality inspection that detected the defect in the first place? Is that work or waste? To answer this question, you must ask another question: Does the quality inspection move the process forward? The answer is no, it really doesn't. However, if the inspection step is eliminated, the quality of the output may suffer. So, is an inspection work or waste?

Technically speaking, an inspection is a non-value adding process step. It's waste. However, we sometimes need such process steps to assure output quality. To minimize the delay and cost of inspections, we should combine them with a value-adding process step. For example, we can combine a value-adding operational step with an inspection step (more about this in Chapter 6).

Example 4

Working as a nurse in a large hospital, you ask a patient to fill out a questionnaire. The patient curtly replies that the same information was requested by the receptionist downstairs. You inform the patient that the receptionist requested information for the Accounts department. You need the same information for your department. When the questionnaire is completed, you politely thank the patient and later during your shift, you enter the information into a computer.

Gathering the same information twice is waste. If we examine the entire patient admission process, gathering the same information a second time is like rework. You're simply repeating a process step.

Entering information into a computer after collecting it on a paper form is also waste (see Figure 2.5). The data entry step is repeated and it does not add value to the process. Capturing information with pen and paper only to enter it into a computer is a common form of waste. Why not enter the information directly into the computer while you're collecting it?

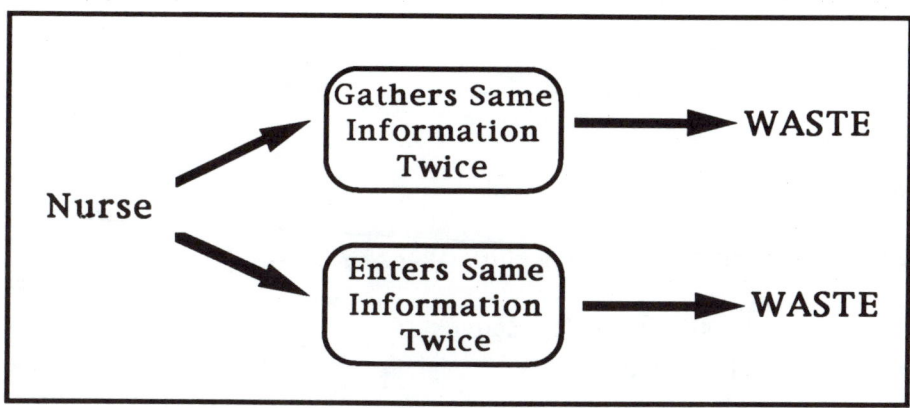

Figure 2.5

Key Point

Whenever possible, collect and enter information once at its source. Collecting the same information twice is a non-value adding activity. Collecting information in one form and then transcribing and reentering it into another form is also a wasteful activity.

Identifying Work and Waste

As described in the preceding examples, waste appears in many forms—needless rework, transportation, delays, inspections, and so on. In each instance, the activity or step does not move the process forward or directly add value. Instead, the activity causes delay and adds cost.

To identify waste, ask yourself the following questions:

- If this particular process activity is eliminated or minimized, will the quality of the output suffer?
- As a customer, am I willing to pay for this particular activity? Is it of value to me?

If the answer is no, the activity is probably waste. Process waste should be eliminated or at least minimized. In the next chapter, we will further distinguish between work and waste. We will also identify specific process steps or activities that fall into each category.

To practice the ideas presented so far, try the following exercise. Remember the meaning of work and waste. Work adds value, waste doesn't. Work moves a process forward, waste doesn't. In addition, remember to ask the following questions:

- Will the quality of the output suffer if this activity is eliminated or minimized?
- Am I willing to pay for this activity?

Exercise

Identify each activity by circling either **Work** or **Waste**.

1	Performing any non-value adding activity	Work	Waste
2	Searching for information	Work	Waste
3	Assembling two components	Work	Waste
4	Repeating a step in a process	Work	Waste
5	Transporting materials	Work	Waste
6	Performing any value-adding activity	Work	Waste
7	Inspecting a part for defects	Work	Waste
8	Waiting for a meeting to begin	Work	Waste
9	Reentering data a second time	Work	Waste
10	Walking to a service van for a part	Work	Waste
11	Storing material in a warehouse	Work	Waste
12	Capturing data once at the source	Work	Waste
13	Performing any rework step	Work	Waste

Work Efficiency

Ideally, all of our work processes contain only work and no waste. Realistically, that's hard to achieve. Instead, we must maximize process work and minimize process waste. Work efficiency provides a useful indication of how successful we are in reaching this goal. Work efficiency is a mathematical expression of the amount of work as opposed to waste—in a process.

Work Efficiency is expressed as:

$$\frac{\text{Work}}{\text{Work} + \text{Waste}} \times 100\%$$

For example, assume that a process can be completed in eight hours. It contains four hours of work or value-adding activities. It also contains four hours of waste or non-value adding activities. The work efficiency of the process is:

$$\frac{4}{4+4} \times 100\%$$

$$= .50 \times 100\%$$

$$= 50\%$$

The ideal work efficiency of any process is 100 percent. The closer we come to that ideal number, the better the process. Unfortunately, we often find processes with a 1 percent to 5 percent work efficiency. Obviously, such processes are leading candidates for process reengineering.

14 | *The Process Reengineering Workbook*

Exercise

For more practice, calculate the work efficiency for the following example. In the example, you must first determine if the activity is work or waste. Then add up the work and waste time columns and plug the totals into the formula.

Activity	Time	Work	Waste
Repair imaging equipment	90	✓	
Walk to service van	12		✓
Search for needed information	6		✓
Walk back to job	12		✓
Repair imaging equipment	75	✓	
Walk to service van	12		✓
Search for needed information	6		✓
Walk back to job	12		✓
Repair imaging equipment	15	✓	

Total Time: _____ _____

Work Efficiency:

$$\frac{\rule{3cm}{0.4pt}}{\rule{1cm}{0.4pt} + \rule{1cm}{0.4pt}} \times 100\% = $$

Process Reengineering

The goal of process reengineering is to decrease the amount of waste in any work process. This in turn increases work efficiency. High work efficiencies are desirable.

As illustrated in Figure 2.6, process improvements can result in:

- More work being accomplished in the same amount of time.
- The same amount of work being accomplished in much less time.

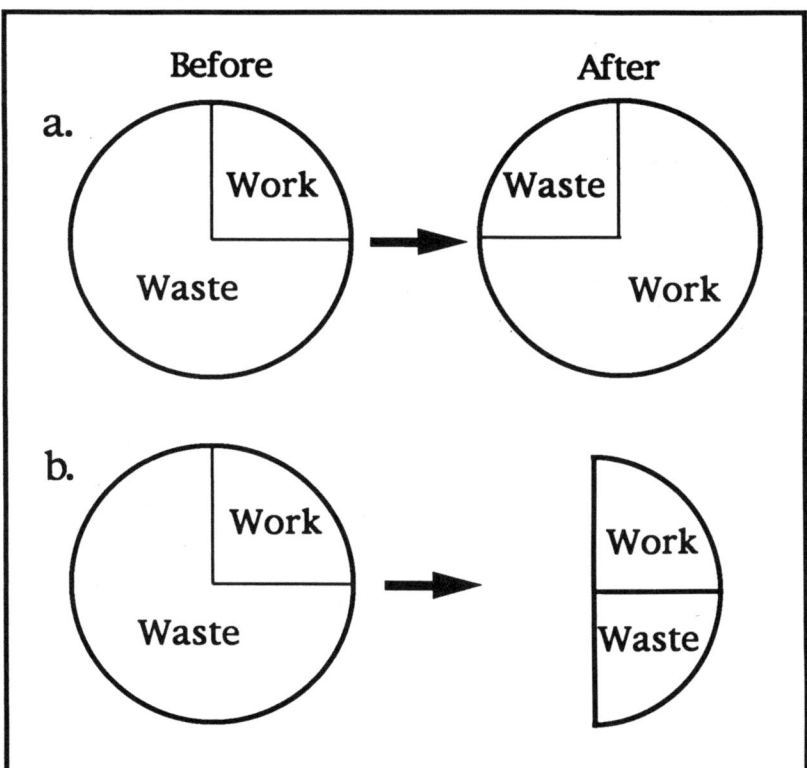

Figure 2.6 Through process reengineering, more work can be done in the same amount of time (a) or the same amount of work can be done in much less time (b).

Can you think of an example where it might be preferable to accomplish the same amount of work in much less time? What if you sometimes work around hazardous, radioactive waste. You certainly want to minimize your exposure time—that is, you want to get in and out of the area as quickly as possible. Doing the same amount of work in much less time accomplishes this goal.

Summary

We can divide the time we spend on the job into *work* and *waste*. Work represents activities that move a process forward. Work directly adds value. Waste represents all non-value adding activities. Waste does not move a process forward. Instead, waste adds only delay and cost.

The goal of process reengineering is to maximize work and minimize waste. Such efforts increase *work efficiency*. Work efficiency is the ratio of work to waste in a process. Ideally, work efficiency is 100 percent.

Successful process reengineering efforts can result in more work being accomplished in the same amount of time. They can also result in the same amount of work being accomplished in much less time.

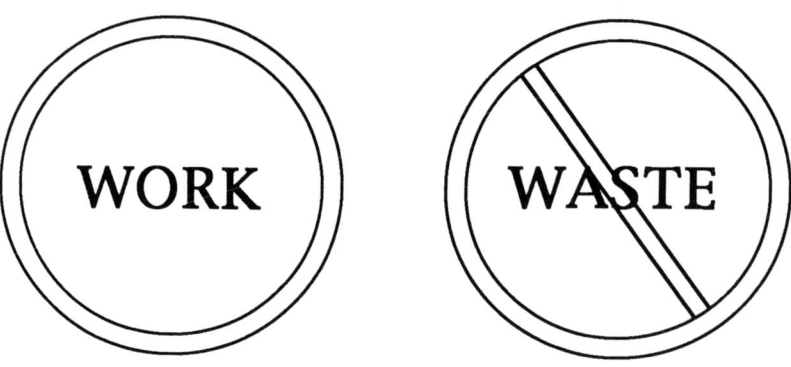

THREE

Work Processes

- A geological exploration crew searches for gold.
- A patient is treated in a hospital.
- A milling machine undergoes routine maintenance.
- A couple is served dinner at a restaurant.
- An insurance claim is processed.
- A computer component is manufactured.
- An engineering design drawing is created.
- A newspaper is published.
- A package is shipped overnight via air express.

At first glance, these activities seem unrelated. Serving dinner at a fancy restaurant has little to do with searching for gold. Creating an engineering drawing can't be related to processing an insurance claim or to shipping an important package. Obviously, these activities are all very different. Or are they?

Although at first glance these activities may seem different, they all represent one thing. They all represent different types of *processes*. And all processes share common characteristics. What's a process?

A process is the blending and transformation of a specific set of inputs into a more valuable set of outputs.

Think about cooking a juicy cheeseburger. The output is the cooked cheeseburger. The inputs are the bun, meat, cheese, lettuce, tomatoes, and onions. The process is preparing the whole thing—slicing the tomatoes, cooking the meat, melting the cheese, and so on. A process transforms a set of inputs into a more valuable set of outputs.

Outputs can involve:

- *Producing a product.* Examples of producing a product include cooking a cheeseburger, filling out a form, and assembling a computer. The cooked cheeseburger, the completed form, and the assembled computer are products.
- *Providing a service.* Examples of providing a service include serving

people at a restaurant, waiting on a customer at a bank, and flying passengers from New York to San Francisco.
- *Completing a task.* Examples of completing a task include changing the filter in a pump, inspecting steel drums containing hazardous chemicals, and capturing an out of control satellite in outer space.

Inputs include many things:

- People.
- Materials.
- Equipment.
- Information.
- Procedures.
- Policies.
- Time.
- Money.

We can depict a process—the transformation of inputs into outputs—as shown in the following flowchart:

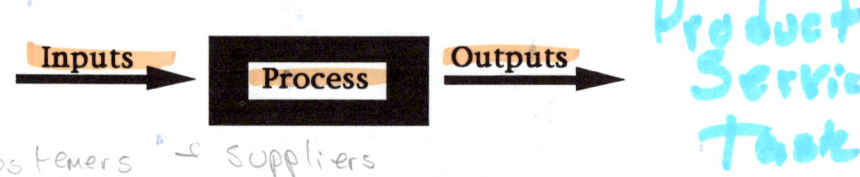

However, our graphical representation of a process isn't quite right. It leaves out two important elements—customers and suppliers.

Outputs go to customers. Customers receive our products or services. There are two types of customers—internal and external. Internal customers work in the same company as we do. External customers work outside our company. When you receive an output—a product or service—from a coworker, you're an internal customer. When you go grocery shopping, you're an external customer.

Key Point

Customers, whether internal or external, are the most important part of any process. Customers purchase or receive our outputs. When they no longer need or want to purchase our outputs, we're in big trouble.

Outputs almost always have some effect on our customers:

- "This is great. It's just what I want."
- "Last time the service was fantastic. This time it's horrible."
- "This won't work. It's not what I wanted."
- "It took too long. I needed it sooner."
- "It costs too much. I can get the same thing cheaper elsewhere."

Sometimes the effect of an output is positive. This results in happy customers. Happy customers are good. Sometimes, however, the effect is negative. When it's negative, we have unhappy customers. Unhappy customers aren't so good.

Successfully satisfying customer needs is what a process is all about. Satisfied customers keep companies in business. Because customers are so important, we need to constantly find out what they think of our outputs. We need to listen to their opinions. Then we need to plug this information, called feedback, back into the process. Customer feedback allows us to constantly improve our outputs.

Suppliers provide some of our inputs. In the cheeseburger example, the grocery store where we buy the ingredients is a supplier. Setting requirements for suppliers is important. We need high-quality inputs if we are to produce high-quality outputs.

Bad inputs can result in bad outputs. The old saying, "garbage in, garbage out," is true. We must control the quality of our inputs just as carefully as we control the quality of our outputs.
Key Point

As illustrated in the following flowchart, a more complete process model includes both suppliers and customers:

A Process Model

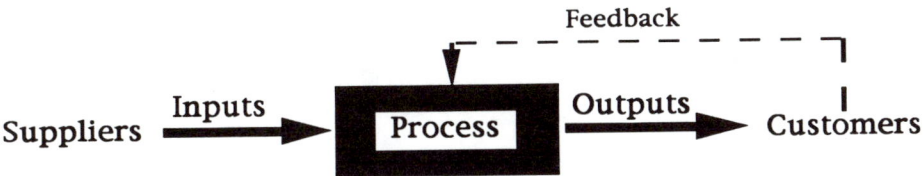

As shown in the model, a process transforms inputs into outputs. Suppliers commonly provide some of the inputs. Customers receive outputs. The goal of any process is to satisfy customers and successfully meet their needs. To satisfy customers, we must continually get feedback about our outputs. Another process goal is to deliver outputs better, faster, and cheaper than our competition.

To think more about inputs, outputs, customers, and suppliers, try the exercise on the next page.

Exercise

Think about a work process that you're involved with. Then answer the following questions.

1. • What are the process outputs?

   Rework.

2. • Do the outputs represent a product, a service, the completion of a task, or some combination?

3. • Who receives the outputs? Who are the customers?

   Internal + External

4. • Are the customers internal or external? Or both?

   Both

5. • What are some of the process inputs?

6. • Who are some of the input suppliers?

   Internal suppliers

Other Process Characteristics

We need to cover a few other points about processes before we open the process black box. Most companies are organized along departmental or functional lines. For example, a typical company has an accounting department, an engineering department, a training department, and so on. Organizing by separate departments or functions creates a functional hierarchy. However, processes don't know about functional hierarchies. They're not very smart. They do stupid things like cut across departments and functions.

As illustrated in Figure 3.1, processes are horizontal and organizations are vertical. Organizations usually look like a bunch of separate smokestacks. Each smokestack represents a separate department, unconnected to any others. Processes are like long pipelines. In a process, everything is connected.

This difference between processes and organizations creates lots of problems. It spawns turf battles, poor communication, and lousy coordination. It also

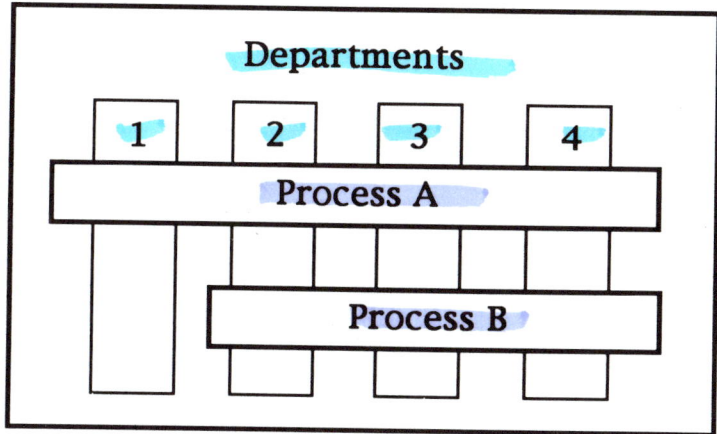

Figure 3.1

results in situations where no one seems to be in control. Everyone owns a piece of the pie, but nobody owns the whole thing. To avoid such confusion, companies are starting to organize along processes. They are learning to manage cross-functionally. When companies organize along processes, neat things begin to happen: communication improves, coordination improves, quality improves, things get done faster, and things get done cheaper.

Sometimes, people divide processes into different levels. For example, processes can be divided into subprocesses. Packaging and crating can be considered a subprocess of the shipping process. Like a process, a subprocess has its own inputs and outputs. The only difference is that the outputs of one subprocess become the inputs for the next subprocess.

For example, a subprocess in a widget manufacturing process might be making widget arms. The output of this subprocess is a widget arm. The output of the making-widget-arms subprocess in turn becomes an input for the widget-assembly subprocess. In one subprocess, the widget arm is an output. In the next, it's an input.

A subprocess can be further divided into a series of activities. In the making-widget-arm subprocess just described, one activity might be to paint the arm. Activities can in turn be divided into a series of steps (see Figure 3.2). More about process steps later.

If you find this type of process division useful, use it. If not, don't. It really isn't important if you're a process splitter or a lumper. What does matter is that you improve the process, not classify it to death!

There is one last point to emphasize about processes. Core process outputs represent real value to a company. Remember, a core process is what a company is all about. Companies are paid for a core process output—a service or a particular product. Companies make money on core process outputs.

However, inputs cost money. So does transforming inputs into outputs.

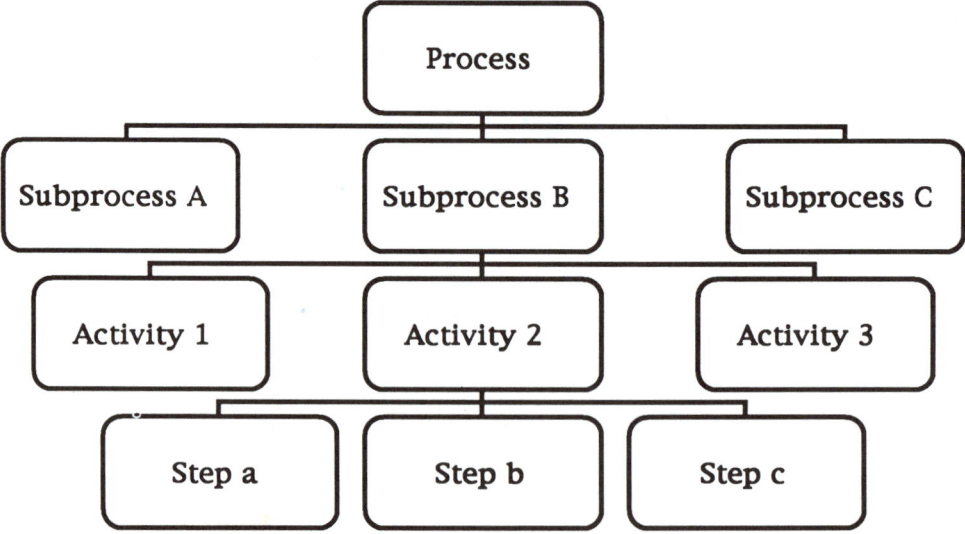

Figure 3.2

That is, the process also costs money. Profit equals the value of the outputs minus the cost of the inputs and the process:

$$\text{Profit} = \text{Output Value} - (\text{Input Costs} + \text{Process Costs})$$

For example, if a product costs $50, the inputs cost $20, and the process costs $25, profit is calculated as follows:

$$\$50 - (\$20 + \$25) = \$50 - \$45 = \$5$$

If process costs increase to $35, however, a $5 loss occurs:

$$\$50 - (\$20 + \$35) = -\$5$$

Why is this idea so important? The value that most companies receive for similar outputs is about the same. To stay competitive, Company A must sell a similar product at about the same price as Companies B, C, and D. That's the way business works.

The cost of inputs is also relatively fixed. Company A will pay about the same price for supplies and materials as Companies B, C, an D. That's also how business works.

It seems then that the only place left to increase profits is in the process. The cheaper the process, the greater the profit. The more expensive the process, the lower the profit. It's really that simple.

Let's look at an example. Two companies, A and B, both located in the same town, make identical widgets. Both companies sell their widgets for $35 a piece. Inputs cost both companies $10. Company A's process costs $20. However, Company B's process costs only $10. Company A's profit is:

$$\$35 - (\$10 + \$20) = \$5$$

Company B's profit is:

$$\$35 - (\$10 + \$10) = \$15$$

Company B's process costs are half those of Company A's. As a result, Company B makes a much higher profit per widget than Company A—$15 versus $5. Which company do you think is more competitive? Which company would you rather work for, Company A or Company B?

Key Point Companies with the lowest process costs usually have the highest profits. That's why eliminating waste in a process is so important. Waste costs money. Waste lowers profits. Eliminating waste allows companies to stay competitive and profitable.

Exercise

Try this example. Two companies, X and Y, offer identical services. Company X charges $40 for their service. Company Y charges $35. Supplies for both companies cost $10. Process costs for Company X are $25. Process costs for Company Y are $15.

- Which company makes the most profit per service call?

    $40 - (\$10 + \$25) = \$5$
    $35 - (\$10 + \$5) = \$10$ Company Y

- By how much?

    $5 dollars

- Which company do you think is the most competitive?

    Company Y

Desired Process Characteristics

The goal of any process is to transform inputs into outputs as effectively, reliably, efficiently, and cheaply as possible (see Figure 3.3). What do these terms—effective, reliable, efficient, and cheap—really mean?

#1 *Effectiveness* refers to the quality of an output; the effect it has on a customer. An effective process meets customer needs. High-quality outputs mean happy customers. Happy customers are good.

#2 *Reliability* refers to consistency of process output; the output quality level is always the same. Have you ever gone to a restaurant and received excellent service and food, then gone back and gotten lousy service but great food, and tried it a third time, only to receive excellent service but lousy food? This is a good example of an unreliable process. If the process was reliable, you'd get great service and food every time.

#3 *Efficiency* commonly relates to process speed; how long it takes to transform inputs into outputs. Cycle time is one expression of process efficiency.

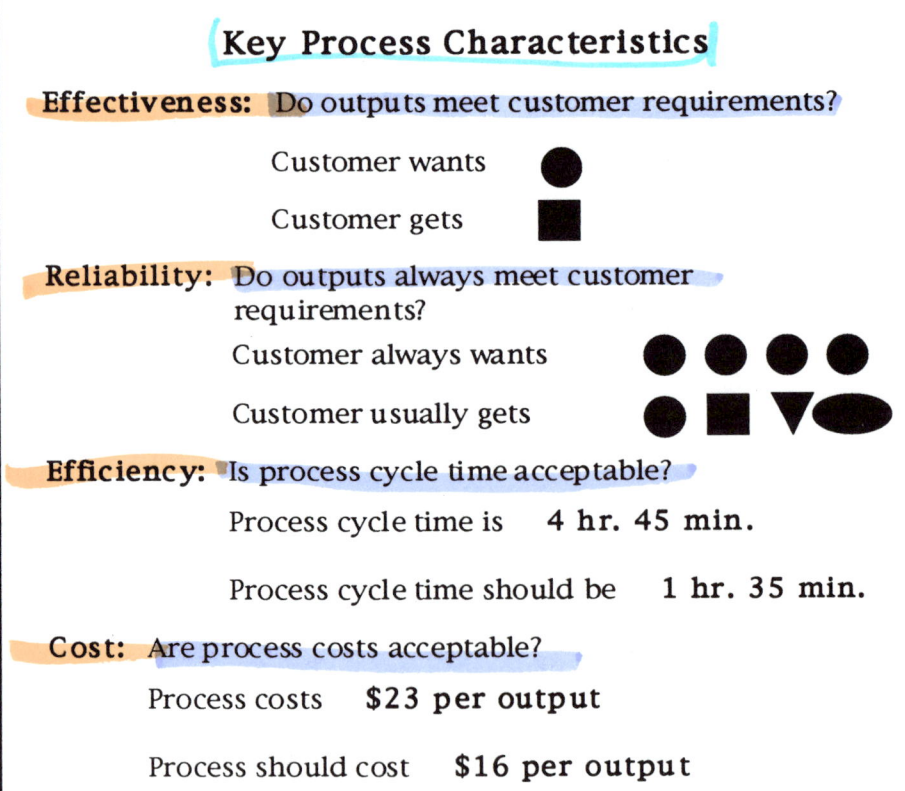

Figure 3.3

Cycle time is the amount of time it takes a process to transform one set of inputs into a set of outputs.

Cheaper refers to the cost of transforming a set of inputs into a set of outputs. The cheaper the process, the higher the profits. Many things affect the cost of a process. One factor is cycle time. The old saying "time is money" is really true. The more delay in a process, the more expensive it is.

The Process Black Box

Most process improvement or quality programs teach basically the same points:

- Listen to customers and give them what they want.
- Develop good relationships with suppliers.
- Constantly improve the process.

This is good advice. But how do we actually improve processes? How do we make work processes better, faster, and cheaper? How do we make the black box called *Process* a little less mysterious? Let's begin by looking inside the box:

A process is the blending and transformation of inputs into outputs. When we transform inputs into outputs, we go through a series of steps. For example, when we make a cheeseburger, we cut the lettuce, fry the meat, melt the cheese, toast the buns, and so on. These steps are called process steps. There are six basic process steps:

1. Operation.
2. Transportation.
3. Inspection.
4. Delay.
5. Storage.
6. Rework.

Think of a widget assembly process. The output is an assembled widget ready for shipping. Let's pretend that you are a widget assembler. Some of your time is spent putting widget parts together. You spend time connecting arms, legs, and heads to widget bodies. This type of assembly step is called an *operational* step. It's a step that is physically changing the shape of the widget output. It's moving the widget assembly process forward. When we think of processes, most of us think of operation steps. Operation steps directly add value to an output. When a grocer successfully scans your milk, that's an operation step. It's moving the check-out-groceries process forward. The symbol for an operation step is a circle.

Operation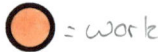

We also move things from one point to another in a process. For example, while assembling widgets, you walk to a parts bin to get some needed parts. Then you return to your workbench with the parts. When you are returning, you are moving both yourself and the widget parts. This moving step is called a *transportation* step. It refers to moving something or changing the location of something. The object being moved can be almost anything, even you.

Remember the field engineer in the last chapter who kept going back and forth to the service van to get information? Walking back and forth is a transportation step. Processes usually contain lots of transportation steps. Faxing information, trucking supplies, or flying passengers from one city to another all are transportation steps. Something—information, supplies, or people—is being moved from one location to another. An arrow symbolizes a transportation step. However, the direction of the arrow, has no meaning:

Transportation ➡

To continue our example, after we assemble the widget, it goes to Quality Control (QC). When the completed widget is physically moving to QC, that's a transportation step. When it's being examined at QC, that's an *inspection* step. Inspection steps include inspecting for both quality and quantity. Inspection steps also can include reviewing things—for example, a completed form or a company report. Inspection steps also can involve authorizing things. Quality and quantity inspections, reviews, and authorizations are all examples of inspection steps. A square symbolizes an inspection step:

Inspection ■

In the widget assembly process, you also spend some time just waiting. This waiting period is also a process step. It's called a *delay* step. Delay steps are unscheduled. For example, when you walk to the parts bin (a transportation step), you might have to wait for an elevator. Or a conveyor belt might break down, causing you to wait while it's being repaired. You might even have to wait on the person supplying widget parts. Each unscheduled waiting period is called a delay.

An object, such as a widget, can also experience delays. For example, after being transported to QC, your assembled widget might sit on a bench for an hour before being inspected. That hour is a delay. A form sitting in an in basket is another good example of a delay step. So is the time spent searching for information or waiting for a meeting to begin. Delays do not move a process forward. They only add time. A stretched D is the symbol for a delay step:

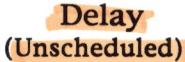

After the widget passes the quality inspection, it goes to a warehouse for storage before final shipping. This scheduled storage period is another type of process step. It's a type of delay step, but it's scheduled, so we call it a *storage* step. Delay steps are unscheduled, storage steps are scheduled. Storage steps usually refer to the storage of objects, not people. Widgets are delayed and stored. People are only delayed, they are not stored. An upside-down triangle is the symbol for a scheduled storage step:

Storage
(Scheduled Delay)

Sometimes during the widget assembly process you make a mistake and have to repeat a step. For example, you might place an arm upside down on a widget. Going back to fix a mistake like this is called *rework*, which is repeating an operational step. Collecting the same data twice is another example of a rework step, as is entering the same data twice into a computer. Rework is usually caused by human error, defective materials or parts, or poorly designed processes. A circle with an R in the middle is the symbol for rework:

Rework

Table 3.1 summarizes the six basic process steps.

Step	Symbol	Description
Operation	○	Any value-adding step. Directly moves a process forward.
Transportation	▶	Any action that moves information or objects, including people.
Delay (Unscheduled)	D	Unscheduled delay of materials, parts, or products. Any human waiting time.
Inspection	□	Includes quality and quantity inspections, reviews, and authorizations.
Storage (Scheduled Delay)	▽	Scheduled delay of materials, parts, or products.
Rework	Ⓡ	Any unnecessary, repeated operational step.

Table 3.1 The basic process steps.

We will use these six basic process steps and their symbols throughout the rest of the book. Try the following exercise. It involves identifying various process steps.

Exercise

Check the correct step type.

Description	○	→	▷	□	▽	®
1. Searching for information.			✓			
2. Assembling two components.	✓					
3. Repeating a step in a process.						✓
4. Moving materials.		✓				
5. Reviewing a report.				✓		
6. Waiting for a meeting to begin.				✓		
7. Reentering data a second time.						✓
8. Walking to a service van.		✓				
9. Faxing information.		✓				
10. Storing material in a warehouse.					✓	
11. Capturing data once at its source.	✓					
12. Performing a QC inspection.				✓		
13. Waiting for a printout.			✓			
14. Authorizing a form request.	✓					
15. Leaving a form in an in basket.			✓		✓	
16. Encountering a scheduled delay.			✓			

Process Symbols

Using the six basic symbols, we can graphically illustrate the steps in any process:

We read a process sequence from left to right, just like a book. This sequence indicates a process containing seven steps. The seven steps are:

1. Operation.
2. Delay.
3. Transportation.
4. Delay.
5. Inspection.
6. Transportation.
7. Storage.

Sometimes a process sequence is drawn vertically. When this happens, we read the sequence from top to bottom: operation, delay, transportation, delay, inspection, transportation, storage:

Different process sequences also can be illustrated graphically. There are five basic process sequences:

- Linear.
- Parallel.
- Convergent.
- Divergent.
- Decision branch.

A linear process is one in which the process steps are sequential. First you do process step 1, then process step 2, then process step 3, and so on. This is an example of a typical linear process.

○ ▷ → ▷ □ → ▽

In this case, step 1 is an operational step, followed by step 2, a delay step, followed by step 3, a transportation step, and so on.

Processes can also occur in parallel. A parallel process involves two subprocesses occurring at the same time. For example, in the widget assembly process, making widget arms and making widget legs are two parallel subprocesses. That is, widget arms and legs are made at the same time. A parallel process is illustrated like this:

○ ▷ → ▷ □ → ▽

○ → ▷ ○ □ → ▽

Subprocess 1 is the top one. Subprocess 2 is the bottom one. They are shown as parallel, occurring at the same time.

Processes can also be convergent. A convergent process contains two or more parallel processes converging or "coming together" into a single linear process. For example, the making-widget-arm and making-widget-leg subprocesses can converge into the assemble-widget subprocess. This merging of two parallel subprocesses into one linear subprocess is called a convergent process. It looks like this:

Processes also can diverge. A divergent process splits from a linear process into two or more parallel subprocesses. For example, cutting out rough stock is a divergent process for the making-widget-arm and making-widget-leg subprocesses. In this example, both the making-widget-arm and making-widget-leg subprocesses use the same outputs from the cutting-out-rough stock subprocess. The outputs of one subprocess are feeding two other subprocesses. A divergent process looks like this:

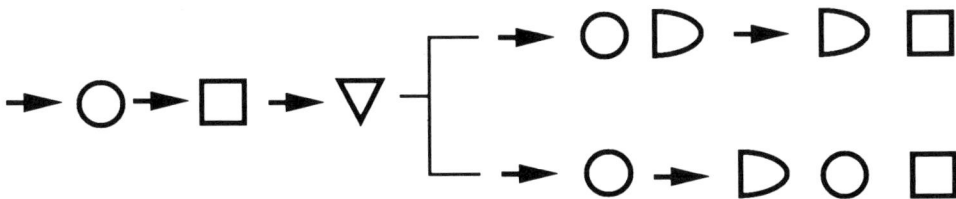

Some processes contain decision points. Based on the decision selected, the process can branch along two or more different paths. Such points are called *decision branches*. The symbol for a decision branch is a diamond:

Decision Point ◇

Let's look at a short example using decision points. The processing of a life insurance application is treated differently depending on an initial medical screening. If the screening is okay, the application is automatically accepted and goes straight to billing. If the screening results are questionable, however, the application follows a second, more complex path. This second path may include additional paperwork and management review and authorization. Such a decision branch process would look like this:

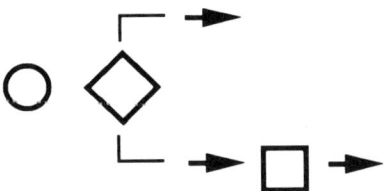

Decision branches can greatly increase the efficiency of a process. Frequently, a process is designed to cover the exception, not the rule. That is, we often design processes to cover 1 percent of the possibilities, not the other 99 percent. With a decision branch, an exception becomes simply an alternative pathway. Decision branches are discussed in greater detail in Chapter 6.

When illustrating processes graphically, it is important to remember that some process steps in a process sequence actually represent mega steps or *activities*. For example, walking from point A to point B is a transportation step.

It's difficult to break down this transportation step further. Even if we did, it wouldn't provide much additional information. Sending something through the mail is also a transportation step. However, this step can easily be broken down into a number of process steps. Thus, mailing is actually an activity. It is a composite of a number of different process steps. This composite idea is illustrated like this:

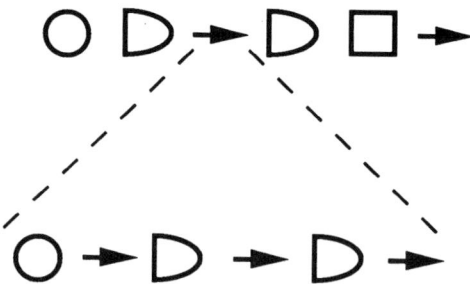

This diagram shows that the transportation step mailing consists of a number of other process steps—operation, transportation, delay, transportation, and so on. Dividing an activity such as mailing often is worthwhile. However, sometimes it's not. We'll cover more about picking the right level later. Just remember, some process analysis is essential. However, too much analysis only wastes valuable improvement time.

A final note: Process steps also can be combined. These process combination steps usually include an operation step combined with an inspection, delay, or transportation step. Combining process steps increases process efficiency. We'll talk more about combining process steps in Chapter 6. Here are some typical process combination symbols:

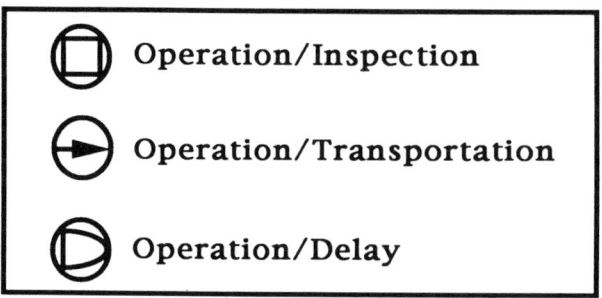

Process Waste

In Chapter 2, we divided the time we spend on the job into *work* and *waste*. Work represents value-adding process steps. Work moves a process forward. Waste represents non-value adding process steps. Waste adds only delay and cost to a process. Remember, the key to improving processes is eliminating or minimizing waste.

If we look at our six process steps—operation, transportation, inspection, delay, storage, and rework—only operational steps directly add value. An operation step moves the process forward. Operational steps represent work, and work is good.

The other five steps—transportation, inspection, delay, storage, and rework—represent waste (see Table 3.2). They add only cost and delay. None of these five steps directly move a process forward. If these steps are eliminated or minimized, the value of the output is usually not affected. In fact, it's almost always increased.

Table 3.2 Only operation steps add value.

Step	Symbol	Work	Waste
Operation	O	X	
Inspection	□		X
Delay (Unscheduled)	D		X
Transportation	→		X
Storage (Scheduled Delay)	▽		X
Rework	Ⓡ		X

Consider the widget assembly process. To get widget parts, you must travel a total distance of 40 feet. Does that 40 feet add value to the widget output? Is output value less if you walk only 20 feet? How about 10 feet? What happens if you don't have to walk to get parts at all? In this case, eliminating the transportation step actually adds value to the output. It decreases process cycle time, and time is money.

However, what happens to output value if you don't put arms on the widget? By eliminating this operational step—assemble arms—output value is decreased. Who wants to buy a widget without arms? Operational steps add value to an output.

In some cases, we can't eliminate a non-value adding step. For example, we can't eliminate the transportation distance between point A and point B. Nor can we make it any less distance. However, we can sometimes minimize the time it takes to get from A to B. More about this later.

To review, there are six basic process steps:

- Operation.
- Transportation.
- Inspection.
- Delay.
- Storage.
- Rework.

Only operational steps represent work. They add value. Operational steps directly move a process forward. The other five steps represent waste. They add only delay and cost. They don't directly move the process forward.

The key to making processes better, faster, and cheaper is to:

- Identify the various types of steps in a process.
- Eliminate or minimize all process steps representing waste.

Remember, waste includes transportation, inspection, delay, storage, and rework steps.

A process analysis is a simple and effective way of identifying and eliminating process waste. Process analysis is the subject of Chapter 4.

Summary

A process is the blending and transformation of a specific set of inputs into a more valuable set of outputs. Ideally, all processes are effective, reliable, efficient, and cheap. Outputs involve: producing a product, providing a service, or completing a task.

Inputs include people, materials, equipment, information, procedures, policies, time, and money. Some inputs are provided by suppliers. Outputs go to either internal or external customers. Customers are the most important part of any process:

A Process Model

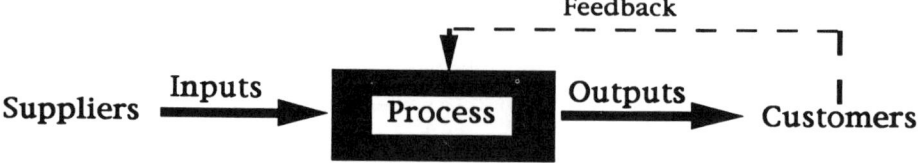

There are six basic steps in any process. These steps are:

1. Operations.
2. Transportation
3. Inspections.
4. Delays.
5. Storage.
6. Rework.

Only operational steps represent work. They add value and directly move the process forward. The other five steps represent waste. They add only delay and cost. The key to process improvement is to eliminate or minimize transportation, inspection, delay, storage, and rework steps.

Process steps can be arranged in a linear, parallel, convergent, divergent, or decision branching manner. Process steps also can be combined. For example, operational steps can be combined with inspection, delay, or transportation steps.

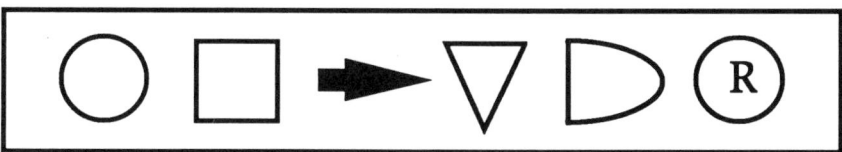

FOUR

Process Analysis and Measurement

"Hi John. How's the widget assembly process doing?"
"Great. Everything is just great."
"That's good. We've eliminated most of the waste then?"
"Oh yeah. There's no waste at all."
"Good. What's the work efficiency?"
"Uh, I don't know."
"Hm. What's the cycle time down to?"
"Don't know."
"What are your process costs?"
"Don't have the slightest idea. But it's a great process!"

There's an old saying:

Without data you're just somebody else with an opinion.

This is so true when it comes to process reengineering. When you ask managers about a process, it's amazing how little they know. What process steps are involved? How much waste exists? What's the work efficiency and cycle time? What does the process cost? Which areas are ripe for improvement? Without this information, it's almost impossible to make significant improvements. To make process improvements we need process-related data.

An easy way to get this needed data is to conduct a process analysis. In this chapter, we'll introduce process analysis. Chapter 5 will cover the nuts and bolts of conducting a systematic process analysis.

A process analysis describes the different types of steps associated with a particular process. It identifies both value-adding (i.e., work) and non-value adding (i.e., waste) process steps. Remember, the key to process reengineering is eliminating or minimizing process waste. Before we can eliminate it or minimize it, however, we must identify it. A process analysis allows you to do just that—identify waste.

A process analysis also lets you examine the overall flow of any labor activity. Processes involve a set of steps, and a process analysis allows you to capture both the types of steps and their specific order.

A process analysis also lets you capture quantitative data, including:

- How long the process takes.
- How much waste it contains.
- How many people are involved.
- What it costs.

Quantitative data is numerical data. For example, if you say process cycle time is 2.5 hours, that's quantitative data. It's a numeric measurement. We call these process-related numeric measurements *metrics*. A metric is a quantitative process measurement. Time, cost, distance, and number of people are all metrics.

However, the purpose of a process analysis is not simply to collect data. Rather, it is to make some type of improvement. Collecting data and then doing nothing with it is a waste of time and effort. The ultimate purpose of any process analysis is to:

- Increase output quality.
- Increase process efficiency.
- Reduce process-associated costs.
- Make work easier and less fatiguing.
- Make work safer.

There are several different types of process analyses. We will focus on two types. One type is called a process task analysis. The other is called a process product analysis (see Figure 4.1).

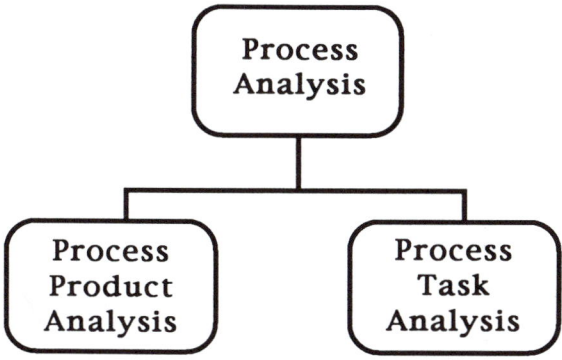

Figure 4.1

A process task analysis focuses on a human activity. A process product analysis focuses on what is being done to an object.

> **In a process task analysis, you're "one" with the human. In a process product analysis, you're one with the object.**

Think of a widget assembly process. We can focus our analysis on what humans are doing to the widgets. We can also focus on the widgets themselves. A process task analysis focuses on what someone is doing in order to assemble widgets. Such process steps may include assembling parts, walking to get parts, searching for needed parts, carrying parts back to a workbench, assembling the new parts, inspecting the assembled widget, and so on.

A process product analysis focuses on the widget and what happens to the widget as it is being assembled. For example, the widget might get arms, travel on a conveyor belt, be delayed while sitting on a workbench, be inspected, be transported to a warehouse, and be stored before shipping.

The process task analysis and the process product analysis both reveal sequences of process steps. We can represent these steps graphically with our process symbols.

The assemble-widget process task analysis identifies what a human does to a widget, and it consists of six steps:

1. Assembling parts.
2. Walking to get parts.
3. Searching for needed parts.
4. Carrying parts back to the bench.
5. Assembling parts.
6. Inspecting assembled parts.

Assembling parts is an operation step. Walking and carrying parts are transportation steps. Searching for needed parts is a delay step. Inspecting assembled parts is an inspection step. Using the proper symbols, the process looks like this:

We can do the same thing for the process product analysis. Remember, a process product analysis focuses on an object. In this case, the object is a widget. The process consists of a widget:

1. Getting arms.
2. Traveling on a conveyor belt.
3. Being delayed while sitting on a bench.

4. Being inspected.
5. Being transported to storage.
6. Being stored before shipping.

Getting arms is an operation step. Traveling on a conveyor belt and being transported are transportation steps. Sitting on a bench is a delay step. Undergoing a quality inspection is an inspection step. Being stored in a warehouse before shipping is a storage step. These six steps look like this:

We can also determine how long each step takes. For example, in the previous assemble-widget process product analysis, getting arms takes 10 minutes, traveling on a conveyor belt takes 5 minutes, and sitting on a bench takes 45 minutes. With this information, we can calculate such useful information as cycle time and work efficiency.

In a rather simple fashion, we've just conducted a process analysis. A process analysis consists of:

- Observing and recording each process step.
- Placing each step in its proper sequence.
- Identifying each type of step.
- Recording all relevant metrics.

To help us do all of these things, we can use a process analysis worksheet. A process analysis worksheet is a simple tool for collecting all the different types of information we need. A blank process analysis worksheet is shown in Figure 4.2.

A process analysis worksheet provides a place to:

- Describe each process step (the Step column).
- Show the step symbol (the Flow column).
- Record an appropriate metric (the Min or minutes column).
- Arrange the step types in their correct order (the Chart Symbol column).

From this information, we can create a data summary chart. A data summary chart summarizes the number of different steps in a process. It also summarizes important quantitative data. A blank data summary chart is shown in Figure 4.3.

To illustrate the proper use of process analysis worksheets and data summary charts, lets look at two examples.

#	Step	Flow	Min	Chart Symbol					
				○	→	▷	□	▽	®
1									
2									
3									
4									
5									
6									
7									
8									
9									
10									

Figure 4.2. A process analysis worksheet is an efficient data collection tool.

Data Summary Chart

Step		Steps	Minutes
Operation	○		
Transportation	▶		
Delay	◘		
Inspection	□		
Storage	▽		
Rework	ⓡ		
Total			

Figure 4.3 A data summary chart simplifies the calculation of such metrics as work efficiency and process cycle time.

Example 1: A Process Task Analysis

Chapter 2 presented several examples illustrating the difference between work and waste. One example described field engineers maintaining and repairing complex hospital imaging and X-ray equipment. To maintain and repair the equipment, the engineers must constantly refer to numerous bulky field manuals and lengthy procedures. These reference materials weigh approximately 150 pounds. They contain some 7,500 pages of information. Because of their weight and size, they are stored on a special shelf in each engineer's service van. To look up needed information, the engineers must make several trips to their service vans each day.

A senior manager at the company wants to know how much this walking back and forth, or transportation step actually costs the company. The company operates throughout the central United States. Maintaining and repairing hospital imaging and X-ray equipment is its core process. The company employs approximately 750 field engineers. The work is highly procedural. One engineer follows essentially the same steps as any other engineer. In other words, the process is essentially the same for all 750 field engineers.

We can answer the question how much does it cost by conducting a simple process analysis. The focus of the analysis is on a human doing something—maintaining and repairing equipment. This requires a process task analysis. Time is used as a process metric. To obtain costs, time is then converted to dollars.

Six field engineers are observed at different job sites across the United States. The observations reveal that the maintaining-and-repairing process consists of the following steps:

42 | *The Process Reengineering Workbook*

- Working on the equipment.
- Walking to the service van.
- Searching for needed information.
- Walking back to the job site.

Those doing the process task analyses are surprised at how similar the process steps are for each field engineer. Combining all six analyses, a typical process task analysis worksheet is created (see Figure 4.4).

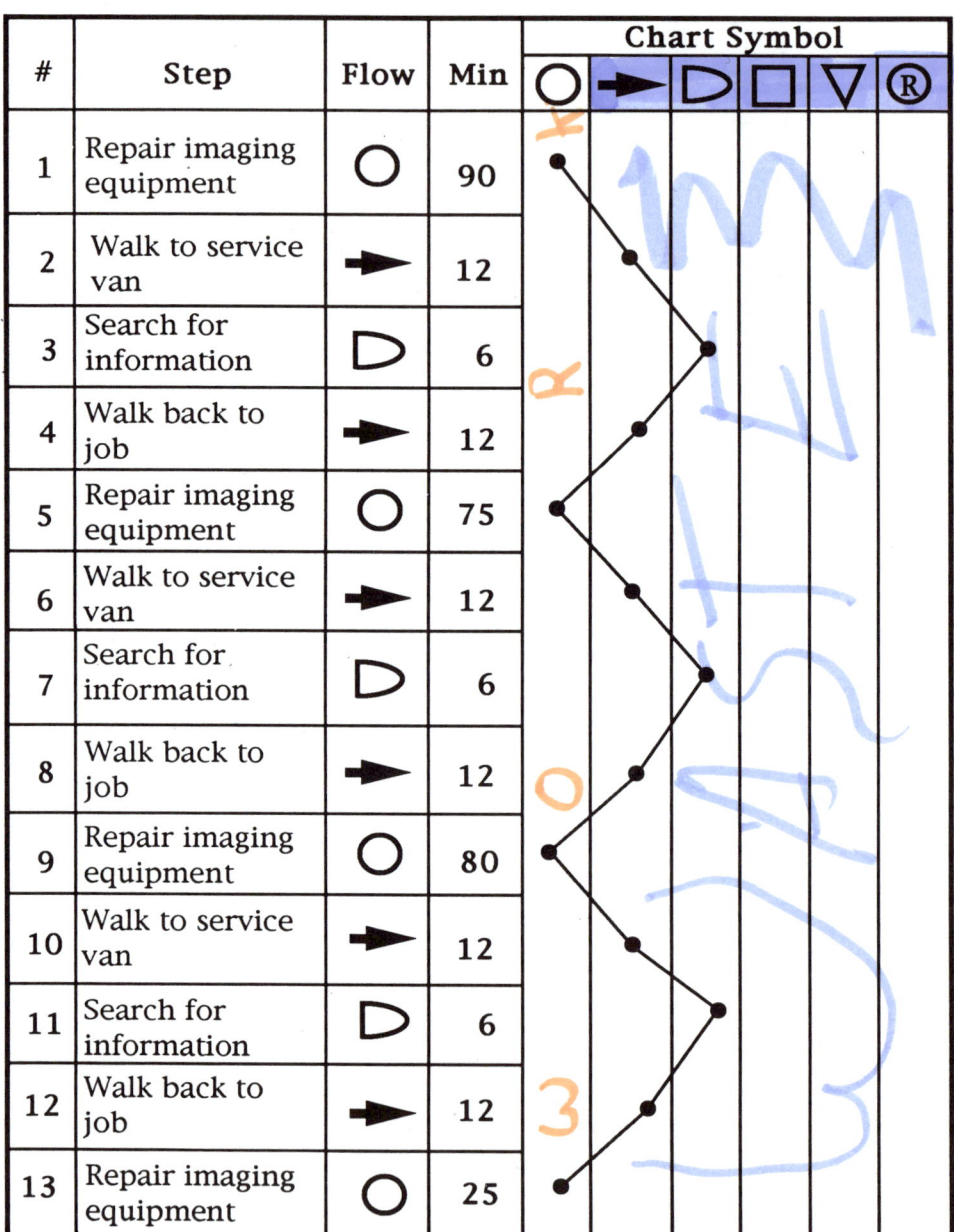

#	Step	Flow	Min
1	Repair imaging equipment	○	90
2	Walk to service van	➔	12
3	Search for information	D	6
4	Walk back to job	➔	12
5	Repair imaging equipment	○	75
6	Walk to service van	➔	12
7	Search for information	D	6
8	Walk back to job	➔	12
9	Repair imaging equipment	○	80
10	Walk to service van	➔	12
11	Search for information	D	6
12	Walk back to job	➔	12
13	Repair imaging equipment	○	25

Figure 4.4

Before we discuss the findings, you should note that we could further subdivide the operation step repair imaging equipment (1, 5, 9, and 13). For our purpose, however, this isn't necessary. When doing a process analysis, it's important to select the right level. In this case, lumping the operation step repair imaging equipment is acceptable.

From the process analysis worksheet, a data summary chart is constructed (see Figure 4.5).

Step		Steps	Minutes
Operation	○	4	270
Transportation	➤	6	72
Delay	D	3	18
Inspection	□		
Storage	▽		
Rework	®		
Total		13	360

Figure 4.5 Data summary chart: repair imaging equipment.

The summary data shows that the average maintaining-and-repairing process contains 270 minutes of work (the operational steps). It also contains 90 minutes of waste (72 + 18 = 90 minutes). From this information, we can calculate work efficiency:

$$\text{Work Efficiency} = \frac{270}{270 + 90} \times 100\% = 75\%$$

Work efficiency is 75 percent. A 75 percent work efficiency means this process has considerable room for improvement.

Now, let's calculate the cost of walking back and forth to a service van. Total transportation time is 72 minutes. Let's assume that a labor hour, or 60 minutes, costs the company $50. This total includes wages, benefits, and overhead. On an average job, 72 minutes, or 1.2 hours, is spent walking (transportation) to get information. This translates into:

$$1.2 \times \$50 = \$60 \text{ per day}$$

Let's also assume there are 208 working days in an average year. Annual transportation costs are:

$$208 \text{ days} \times \$60 = \$12{,}480 \text{ per year}$$

The company pays $12,480 for field engineers to walk back and forth to their service vans. That's $12,480 of waste. That's the "good" news. Now for the really bad news!

Because there are 750 field engineers, we have to multiply $12,480 by 750:

$$750 \text{ engineers} \times \$12{,}480 = \$9{,}360{,}000 \text{ per year}$$

A whopping $9,360,000 of waste! The transportation step—walking back and forth to van—costs the company more than $9 million dollars annually. And when we ask ourselves what value the step adds, the answer is none. Using the information adds value. Getting the information doesn't. In fact, getting the information costs even more than the $9.36 million already calculated. We haven't added in the delay step, searching for information. Let's do that also.

On an average job, 18 minutes (6 + 6 + 6 = 18), or 0.3 hours, is spent searching for information. Delay costs are:

$$0.3 \times \$50 = \$15 \text{ per day}$$

Using 208 working days in an average year, we can calculate annual costs:

$$208 \text{ days} \times \$15 = \$3{,}120$$

The company pays $3,120 for each field engineer to search for information. That's $3,120 of waste.

We can now calculate the annual cost of each field engineer searching for information. It is:

$$\$12{,}480 \text{ (transportation)} + \$3{,}120 \text{ (delay)} = \$15{,}600$$

Total company costs for all 750 field engineers getting information are:

$$\$15{,}600 \times 750 \text{ engineers} = \$11{,}700{,}000$$

Some $11.7 million of waste is associated with the non-value adding task getting information. In Chapter 5 we will revisit this example. We'll show how the transportation step—walking back and forth to van—can be eliminated. We'll also show how the delay step—searching for information—can be minimized. Remember, process reengineering is all about eliminating and minimizing waste.

This example shows how costly waste can be for a company. Walking back and forth to a service van to look up information may seem like a trivial action. It's just part of the job, right? But it costs the company almost $12 million every year! A process analysis lets us identify these so-called trivial actions and begin to eliminate or minimize them.

Key Point Few, if any companies intentionally throw away millions of dollars. Without realizing it, however, companies waste millions and millions of dollars every year. Much of this waste is associated with little things that we never think about or that we don't think really matter. A process analysis lets us identify these little things. Once identified, we can begin to eliminate them or minimize them.

Example 2: A Process Product Analysis

A large company is having trouble processing requisition forms for supplies and materials. Just getting through the initial approval process seems to take forever. Then, the order must be placed, and the supplies and materials must be received and delivered to the correct location.

These delays usually cause only minor inconveniences. However, a lack of supplies and materials sometimes stops an entire operation. After one such instance, a senior manager has had enough. The manager wants to know the reason for the excessive delays. The manager also wants to know who to blame for the problem.

A process analysis is done. The requisition process is broken down into three subprocesses:

- Requisition form completion and authorization.
- Ordering.
- Receiving and delivery.

Let's focus on the first subprocess, requisition form completion and authorization; the req subprocess for short. The output of the req subprocess is a completed and approved requisition form. The completed form is an object. Because the analysis deals with an object, a process product analysis is performed. Because time is of interest, time is used as a metric.

A series of requisition forms are tracked through the system. However, it's difficult to physically watch a form being processed:

"Hi, what did you do today?"

"Oh not much. Just stood around and watched a form sit in an in basket all day. It was pretty exciting."

To avoid this type of excitement, we can use a traveler. A traveler is simply a recording log. It allows people to record various process step types and times. We'll have more to say about travelers in Chapter 5.

After collecting several travelers, a representative process analysis worksheet is developed. Interestingly, all collected travelers look about the same. The process analysis worksheet is shown in Figure 4.6.

#	Step	Flow	Min	Chart Symbol ○	→	D	□	▽	®
1	Requisition form initiated	○	10	•					
2	Form mailed to Procurement	→	720		•				
3	Form sits in in basket	D	75			•			
4	Requisition form completed	○	18	•					
5	Form sits in out basket	D	75			•			
6	Form mailed to Authorization	→	720		•				
7	Form sits in in basket	D	45			•			
8	Form reviewed & authorized	□	12				•		
9	Form sits in out basket	D	90			•			
10	Form mailed to Ordering	→	720		•				

Figure 4.6

Note that transportation steps 2, 6, and 10—Form mailed— can be subdivided further. This activity is actually composed of several process steps. For our purpose, however, little is gained by such division. Once again, it's important to pick the right level for any process analysis.

The process product analysis reveals that the req subprocess contains ten steps: two operational steps, one inspection step, four delay steps, and three transportation steps. Total times for each step type are shown in the data summary chart in Figure 4.7.

The data summary chart shows that the average req subprocess takes 2,475 minutes, or 41.25 hours. The process contains 28 minutes of work and 2,447 minutes of waste (2,160 + 275 + 12 = 2,447 minutes). Work efficiency is 1 percent:

$$\text{Work Efficiency} = \frac{28}{28 + 2447} \times 100\% = 1\%$$

You may be surprised by the low work efficiency. However, for many administrative processes, such low work efficiencies are not uncommon. Some companies experience work efficiencies as low as 0.01% in their administrative processes.

Step		Steps	Minutes
Operation	○	2	28
Transportation	▶	3	2160
Delay	D	4	275
Inspection	□	1	12
Storage	▽		
Rework	Ⓡ		
Total		10	2475

Figure 4.7 Data summary chart: requisition form.

Some important lessons can be learned from this example. The process is terribly inefficient, but the operation is fairly efficient, taking only 28 minutes. When we think of processes, most people consider only operational steps—what people do to something. As shown in this example, such steps are usually only the tip of the iceberg. It's all the other process steps—transportation, delay, inspection, and rework—that make processes so inefficient.

In addition, focusing on finding who to blame won't improve the req subprocess much. If we get people to work twice as fast, we can save only 20 minutes: 14 minutes from the operational steps and 6 minutes from the inspection step. However, if we cut delay and transportation steps by half, we save 1,361 minutes, or 22.7 hours (see Figure 4.8).

If we cut	Then we go from
Operation and inspection steps by half	41.25 hours to 40.9 hours
Transportation and delay steps by half	41.25 hours to 21.0 hours

Figure 4.8

This is why companies need to focus on the *what*, not the *who*. Improving the *what* almost always buys so much more than improving the *who*.

Key Point

When we talk about process reengineering, we usually think about manufacturing processes—that is, processes that involve making something. We typically ignore other processes, such as administrative or routine service processes. However, it is these types of processes that often need the most help. To be competitive, companies must improve all processes.

Process Analysis Significance

As illustrated by these two examples, a great deal can be learned by conducting a process analysis. Some real surprises are usually discovered, along with considerable waste that must be eliminated or greatly reduced.

A process analysis also replaces opinion with fact. It can provide specific measurements of process performance, not just opinions such as "I think it's great!"

To practice process analysis, try the exercise on the following page. Remember, a process analysis consists of:

- Observing and recording each process step.
- Placing each step in the proper sequence.
- Identifying each type of step.
- Recording all relevant metrics.

Armed with this information, we can create a data summary chart. With a data summary chart, we can calculate such useful metrics as work efficiency, cycle time, and process costs. And armed with this information, we can start making significant process improvements. But we'll get to the improvement part in Chapters 5 and 6.

Exercise

To practice doing a process analysis, let's revisit the opening conversation of this chapter. Remember, it went like this:

> "Hi John. How's the widget assembly process doing?"
> "Great. Everything is just great."
> "That's good. We've eliminated most of the waste then?"
> "Oh yeah. There's no waste at all."
> "Good. What's the work efficiency?"
> "Uh, I don't know."
> "Hm. What's the cycle time?"
> "Don't know."
> "What are your process costs?"
> "Don't have the slightest idea. But it's a great process!"

Let's see if we can't do a better job answering these questions than John did.

After talking to John, Bill Acme, the owner of Acme Widget Co., gets a bit uneasy. He wanted John to give him specific process-related data, not just a bunch of opinions. Realizing that something needs to be done, he hires you as a consultant. He wants to know:

- What is the work efficiency of the widget assembly process?
- What is the process cycle time?
- What are the labor costs?

He also wants to see a completed process analysis worksheet and data summary chart.

Accepting the assignment, you observe the widget assembly process several times. You also time each step. The steps and average associated times, placed in the correct sequence, are:

1. Walk to parts bin (2 minutes).
2. Search for legs (1 minute).
3. Carry legs back to workbench (2 minutes).
4. Attach legs (5 minutes).
5. Walk to parts bin (2 minutes).
6. Search for arms (1 minute).
7. Carry arms back to workbench (2 minutes).
8. Attach arms (3 minutes).
9. Walk to parts bin (2 minutes).
10. Search for head (1 minute).
11. Carry head back to workbench (2 minutes).
12. Attach head (2 minutes).
13. Do a quality check on assembled widget (2 minutes).
14. Carry widget to assembled widget bin (3 minutes).

A labor hour, including all associated costs, is $40.
In the spaces provided on the following pages:

- Fill in the process analysis worksheet.
- Fill in the data summary chart.
- Calculate work efficiency.
- Calculate process cycle time.
- Calculate total labor costs per widget assembly.
- Calculate total waste costs per widget assembly.
- Answer the question: *"How's the widget assembly process doing?"*

#	Step	Flow	Min	○	→	D	□	▽	®
1	Walk to Parts Bin.	D	2			•			
2	Search for Legs	D	1			•			
3	Carry legs Back to work bench	→	2		•				
4	Attach legs.	○	5	•					
5	Walk to Parts Bin.	D	2			•			
6	Search for Arms	D	1			•			
7	Carry arms Back to Work Bench.	→	2		•				
8	Attach arms	○	3	•					
9	Walk to Part Bin.	D	2			•			
10	Search for Head.	D	1			•			
11	Carry head Back to Work Bench.	→	2		•				
12	Attach head	○	2	•					
13	Do a quality check on widget	□	2				•		
14	Carry widget to assembled widget bin.	→	3		•				

Chart Symbol

Data Summary Chart

Step		Steps	Minutes
Operation	○	3	10
Transportation	➤	4	9
Delay	D	6	9
Inspection	□	1	2
Storage	▽		
Rework	ⓡ		
Total		14	30

Work Efficiency: $\frac{W}{W+T} \times 100 \qquad \frac{10}{10+20} \times 100\% =$

Process Cycle Time: 30 min.

Total Labor Costs: .5 hr × $40.00 = $20.00

Total Waste Costs: .33 hr × $40.00 = $13.20

"How's the widget assembly process doing?" Doing poorly.

Summary

To significantly improve a process, we must first learn something about it. That something can be learned through a *process analysis*. A process analysis describes all the different types of steps associated with a particular process. It identifies both value-adding (i.e., work) and non-value adding (i.e., waste) process steps. It also collects important process-related *metrics*. A metric is a quantitative process measurement.

The goals of process analysis include:

- Increasing output quality.
- Increasing process efficiency.
- Decreasing process-associated costs.
- Making work easier and less fatiguing.
- Making work safer.

Two types of process analyses can be used (see Figure 4.9). One type is called a *process task analysis*. The other is called a *process product analysis*. A process task analysis focuses on a human activity. A process product analysis focuses on what is being done to an object.

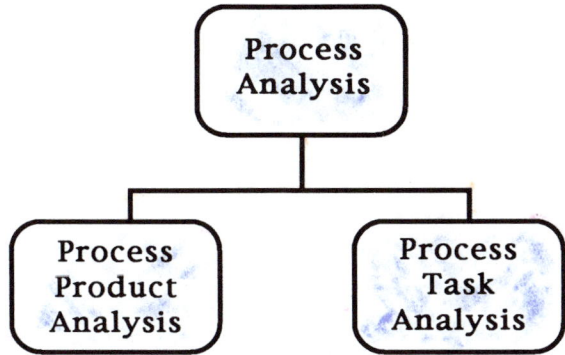

Figure 4.9

Both types of process analyses consist of:

- Observing and recording each process step.
- Placing each step in the correct sequence.
- Identifying each type of step.
- Recording all relevant metrics.
- Summarizing all collected data.

A *process analysis worksheet* and a *data summary chart* are two helpful items for conducting a process analysis. A process analysis worksheet provides a place to:

54 | *The Process Reengineering Workbook*

- Describe each process step.
- Show the correct step symbol.
- Record appropriate metrics.
- Sequence all step types in their correct order.

A data summary chart summarizes the number of different steps in a process. It also summarizes important quantitative data, including time, distance, and number of people.

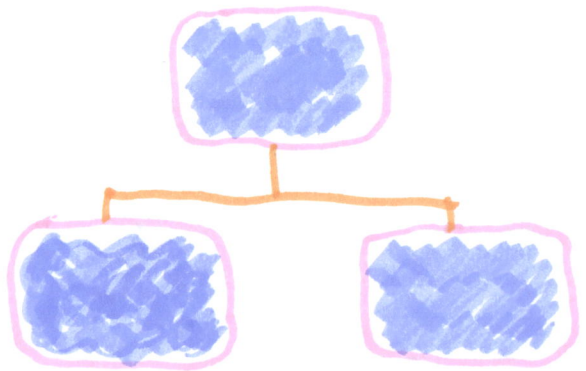

FIVE

The Seven-Step PI Method

Many process reengineering and improvement efforts fail. Why? Because there's no plan. There's no method to the madness. People are guided only by an "I think so." Improvements are opinion-based, not fact-based.

People also chase the trivial many—the little things that don't add up to much—yet they miss the really big things. They miss things that cost companies millions of dollars; things that if changed, can significantly improve performance; things that can enhance quality, shorten cycle times, and decrease costs, as well as make work easier, safer, and less demanding.

To avoid such failures, we need a method—that is, a systematic way of doing process reengineering. We need a method that can provide quantifiable results, help us quickly identify needed areas of improvement, fix what's broken, and reduce waste from the workplace.

Our method is called the process improvement method. Because process improvement method is a bit long, we'll shorten it to the PI method. PI stands for process improvement. Our method contains seven steps, so we'll call the whole thing the Seven-step PI method.

The seven steps of the PI method shouldn't be confused with our six basic process steps. That's something different. Remember, the process steps are operation, transportation, delay, inspection, rework, and storage. The seven steps of the PI method are different. They are:

1. Define process boundaries.
2. Observe process steps.
3. Collect process-related data.
4. Analyze collected data.
5. Identify improvement areas.
6. Develop improvements.
7. Implement and monitor improvements.

The method is simple and easy to follow. It works like this:

1. First you identify a process or part of a process that you want to improve. Then, you define the process boundaries—that is, where

the process begins and where the process ends. You also identify outputs, and you select the relevant metrics.
2. Next, you observe all process steps, including what actually takes place and what the process flow is. While you are observing all of this, you also record your findings.
3. Either during or after the observation phase, you also collect all relevant process-related quantitative data. Remember, we call quantitative process data a metric.
4. After collecting the data, you analyze it and summarize it. In other words, you figure out what it means and how it's significant.
5. From the analyzed data, you identify areas for improvement. You go after the big hitters first. After that, you start on the smaller stuff.
6. Once you know what you want to improve, you develop some type of improvement method. You develop a cure for the ailment.
7. After you've come up with a fix, you implement it. You try it out. During this trial period, you also monitor the improvement to determine how well it's doing.

That's it, seven simple steps. We'll discuss each step in some detail. Then we'll consider two examples that show how the method actually works. First, there are a few points to consider:

- The seven-step PI method can be used by an individual or by a team, though process improvement teams usually are more effective. Two or more heads really are better than one, especially if some of the heads work in the process. If teams are used, however, it's strongly suggested that they receive training before starting the process improvement effort. Training should consist of learning about processes and how to improve them. It should also include some team training. Many process improvement teams fail because they lack effective team and interpersonal skills. Getting along and working as an effective team are often-overlooked elements of process reengineering. So, don't forget the team stuff.
- Using the seven-step PI method shouldn't take forever. Taking months and months to improve a process isn't what process reengineering is all about. Instead, it's all about making improvements now, not months down the road. The cycle time of the complete seven-step PI method should be measured in a few weeks, not months. To get this kind of result, it's important to select the correct process size or bite.
- In selecting processes to improve, go after the biggies first. A 30 percent gain in a process that costs $10 million is more beneficial than a 30 percent gain in a process that costs $10,000. Make process reengineering pay for itself. Go after big gains first.
- When launching process reengineering efforts, companies often set goals in such terms as saving so much money per year, cutting cycle time by

so many days or hours, or eliminating so many defects per 1,000 parts. Frequently, such goals are fairly small—on the order of 3 percent to 5 percent. Don't follow this trend. Go for the gold. Set big goals—what we call *stretch goals*. Goals are on the order of 20 percent to 50 percent. Setting stretch goals forces a company to really look at its processes.
- Finally, don't overlook organizational and management considerations. Such considerations are beyond the scope of this book, as is team training. However, you need to make sure you don't overlook them.

The Seven-Step PI Method

Step 1. Define process boundaries. To improve a process, you first have to select one. That's what Step 1 is all about, selecting a candidate process or subprocess. Step 1 also involves defining process boundaries (i.e., where the process begins and where the process ends). It also includes identifying outputs and inputs.

For example, the widget assembly process begins with getting widget parts and it ends with an assembled widget ready for shipping. The output is an assembled widget. Inputs include widget arms, head, legs, and body.

Any process is a candidate for reengineering. Suggestions for selecting an appropriate process include:

- Go after the big hitters first; choose processes that cost lots of money, take too long, or have serious quality problems.
- Select the right level. Reengineering the manufacturing process or the entire procurement process may be too much. Break big processes down into manageable chunks. For example, instead of trying to reengineer the processing of all forms, select one form. Knowledge gained from that experience can then be applied to other forms. Start small and grow big is a good rule to follow. It usually increases the probability of success, and nothing breeds future success like past success.
- Select processes that cycle within an acceptable time frame. Cycle time should be measurable in hours or days. Processes that stretch out over long periods of time are difficult to track and analyze. Once again, keep things fairly tight. If necessary, break down big processes into more manageable chunks.

After a process is selected, become familiar with it. Discuss it. Read about it. Casually walk it down.

> • • • **CAUTION** • • •
>
> When you start talking to people about a process, everyone has an opinion about what's wrong. Sometimes these opinions can be very useful information. However, such opinions usually are not supported by any hard data. Also, opinions about the real problem rarely point out the real problem. Find out the facts for yourself.

You also must determine the purpose of the process analysis in Step 1. Is the goal to:

- Increase process efficiency by shortening process cycle time?
- Decrease process-related costs?
- Improve output quality or reliability?
- Make work safer?
- Make work easier and less frustrating?
- Achieve some desired combination of the preceding goals?

> • • • **CAUTION** • • •
>
> If the intent of the analysis is to increase process efficiency, first make sure the process is effective and reliable. It does little good to make an ineffective or unreliable process more efficient. The only thing that is accomplished is that the process can now produce defective outputs even faster!

Once the purpose of the process analysis is determined, select appropriate metrics. For example, if the purpose is to shorten cycle time, time is an obvious metric. Distance also may be a useful metric for cycle time. Physically shortening the distance between two process steps can help reduce cycle time. If the purpose is to improve quality, a useful metric might be the number of defects associated with specific process steps.

Sometimes, a required metric cannot be captured directly. For example, assume that you want to calculate labor costs associated with a certain type of process step. To calculate such costs, however, you will probably have to first collect data in terms of time and then convert labor time into labor costs.

In selecting an appropriate metric, use some common sense. Collecting everything about a process may be nice, but it takes time. Select metrics that you can use, including time, number of defects, number of people, distance, and costs.

Finally, you must determine the type of process analysis to conduct. Do you need to conduct a process task analysis, a process product analysis, or both?

Step 1 of the seven-step PI method is a getting started step. It sets the direction for the next six steps. At the end of Step 1, you should have:

- Identified the candidate process.
- Determined process beginning and end.
- Identified process outputs and inputs.
- Identified the purpose of the process analysis.
- Selected appropriate metrics.
- Determined the type of analysis (i.e., task or product).
- Gained general process familiarity.

Step 2. Observe process steps. After the preliminaries are completed, it's time to observe the process. It's important to emphasize the word *observe*. It's a very important part of the process improvement effort.

Many process improvement efforts consist of people going off in some corner and flowcharting what they think a process should be, or what they think it is. Unfortunately, a process is almost always different than what it should be or what we think it is. When people describe a process without actually observing it, they almost always leave things out. For example, they might overlook all of the important non-value adding steps, including transportation, delay, inspection, storage, and rework. For example, if someone described the widget assembly process, it would probably sound like this:

> *"It's pretty simple. First you stick the legs on. Then the arms. Then finally the head. Then you do a quick QA check and throw it in the assembled widget bin. That's it!"*

Three of the described steps are operational. One is an inspection step. This is a good description of the widget assembly operation. However, it does not describe the process. To gain that information, you must observe the process.

You can use many observational techniques. For example, you can physically watch a process. You can also record a process with a video camera. Or, you can use a traveler. Remember, a traveler is simply a form for recording process step information. We'll show an example of a traveler later in this chapter.

> • • • **CAUTION** • • •
>
> Always brief anyone before you observe them. Explain exactly what you are doing and why. Also, assure the individuals that you are not on a spy mission or attempting to get them to work faster. The focus of the observation is on the *what*, not the *who*.

If possible, observe a process more than once. This will give you a better picture of the real process.

During Step 2, you should:

- Identify and record all steps in the process.
- Make a short description of each step.
- Arrange each step in its correct order (i.e., Step 1, Step 2, Step 3).
- Identify each process step by type (e.g., operation, transportation, inspection).

As described in Chapter 4, a process analysis worksheet is a useful tool for recording this information. A process analysis worksheet for the assemble-widget process is shown in Figure 5.1.

Note how different the observed widget assembly process is from the described process. Remember the description?

> *"It's pretty simple. First you stick the legs on. Then the arms. Then finally the head. Then you do a quick QA check and throw it in the assembled widget bin. That's it!"*

According to the described process, there are:

- Three assembly or operational steps.
- One inspection step.

However, when we actually observe the process, a very different picture emerges. We find several other process steps that represent waste. Observing a process usually provides much different information than simply listening to someone describe it.

A process analysis worksheet is an excellent tool to use in Step 2. It provides a well-structured method for collecting the correct information. Depending on the situation, you also might want to create a process overhead view diagram. A process overhead view diagram is a bird's-eye sketch of a process. The orientation is looking down from above. A process overhead view diagram is useful in settings that don't cover a great deal of distance (e.g., some manufacturing and office settings). A process overhead view diagram should be used in addition to a process analysis worksheet.

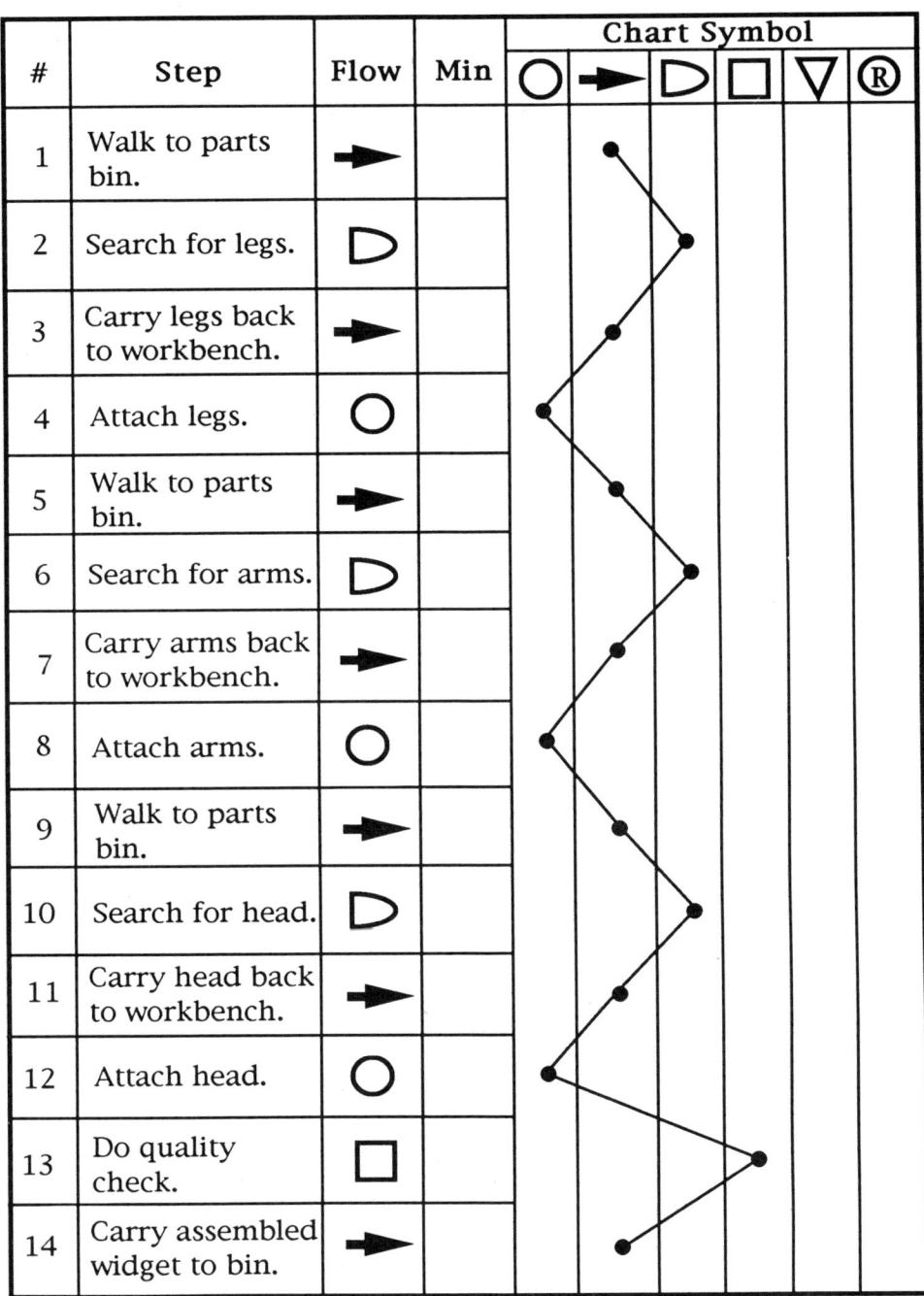

Figure 5.1

62 | *The Process Reengineering Workbook*

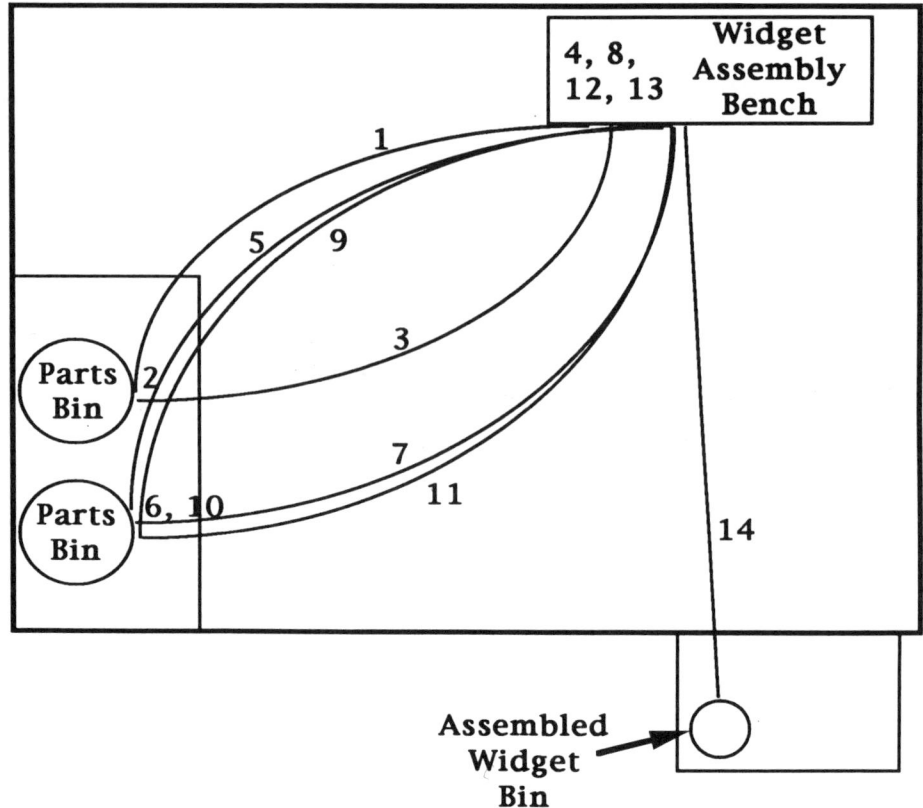

Figure 5.2 Process overhead view diagram.

A process overhead view diagram of the assemble-widget process is illustrated in Figure 5.2.

As shown, a process overhead view diagram is simply a map of the process. It shows where each process step takes place. It also illustrates what happens between the steps. The numbers on the process overhead view diagram correspond to the step numbers on the process analysis worksheet. That's why the two techniques should be used together. As needed, you can add information to the process overhead view diagram. For example, you might want to add actual distances associated with each transportation step, or the number of people working at each station.

Another useful tool is a process flow diagram. A process flow diagram illustrates the overall process flow or sequence. Each step type is depicted in its proper sequence. Process flow diagrams are particularly useful for illustrating parallel, divergent, convergent, or decision branching processes.

A process flow diagram for the assemble-widget process looks like this:

Process Flow Diagram

Step 2 is one of the most important steps of the seven-step PI method. Understanding what a process looks like is essential to successful process reengineering. At the end of Step 2, you should have a good picture of the process. This picture includes the identification and correct sequencing of all process steps. At the completion of Step 2, you should have:

- Observed all process steps.
- Recorded all process steps.
- Identified the process flow and sequence.
- Categorized all process step types.

Step 3. Collect process-related data. Observing and identifying all steps associated with a process is extremely important. However, it's not quite enough. To support our observations, we also need such quantitative data as time, number of people, distance, and number of defects. When we combine Steps 2 and 3, we really have something.

At the end of Step 1, you selected relevant metrics. Now in Step 3, you simply collect them. Sometimes, Steps 2 and 3 are combined. For example, if you are observing a process, it often makes sense to collect metrics at the same time that you collect other needed information.

> ### • • • CAUTION • • •
> It is often best to observe a process a few times before collecting quantitative data. By waiting a bit, more accurate numbers are usually obtained.

If you've videotaped a process, you might want to review the tape and identify the process sequence and type of each step before you collect the metrics. If you use a traveler, you will probably want to combine Steps 2 and 3.

At the end of Step 3, your process analysis worksheet is complete. All columns, including the metric column, are filled out. A completed process analysis worksheet for the assemble-widget process is illustrated in Figure 5.3.

64 | *The Process Reengineering Workbook*

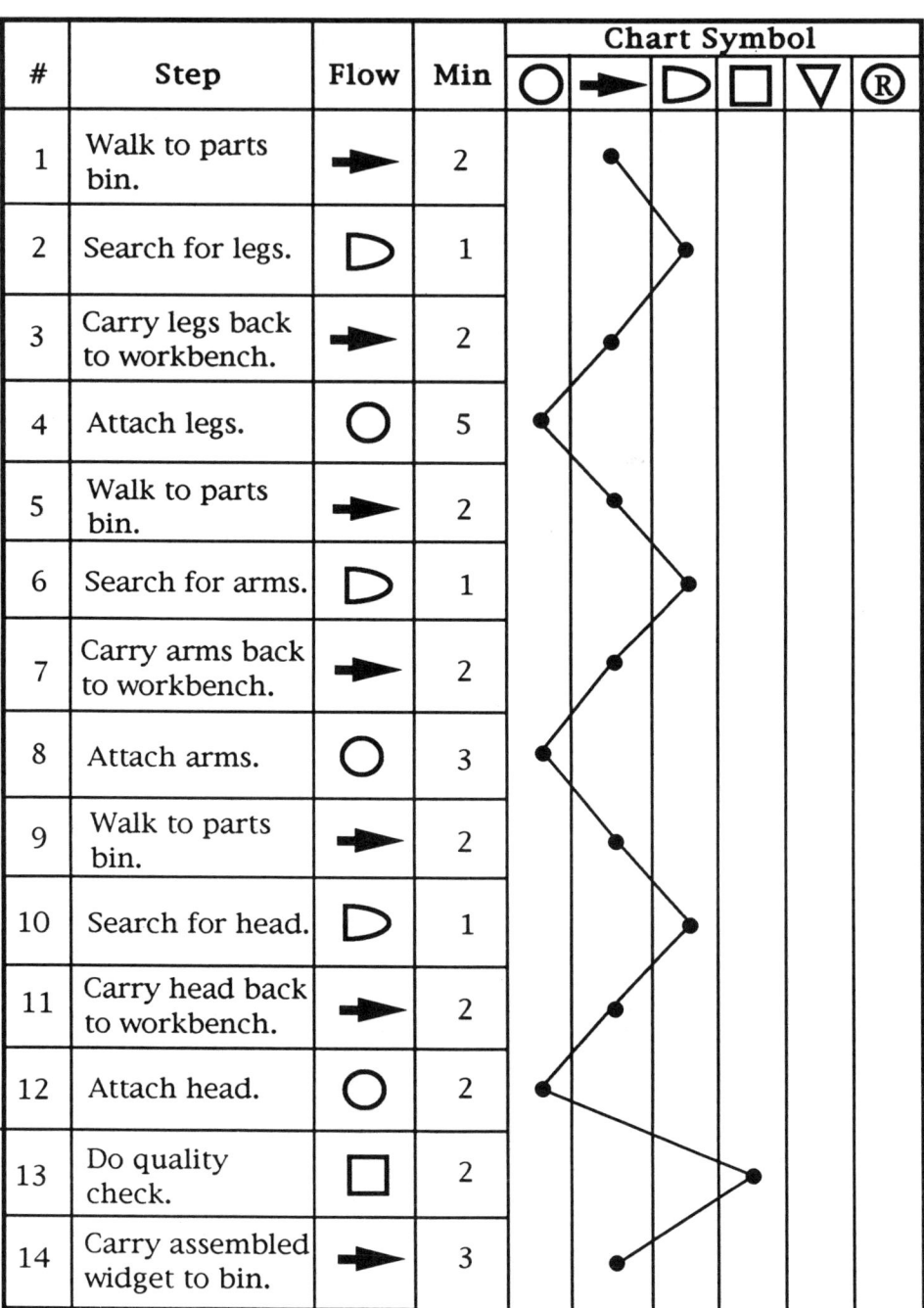

Figure 5.3

To summarize, Step 3 provides all of the quantitative data that is so important in process reengineering. Armed with this type of data, we can replace opinion with hard fact. At the end of Step 3, you have:

- Calculated all process metrics.
- Recorded the metrics on a process analysis work sheet.

Step 4. Analyze collected data. Once all of the data in Steps 2 and 3 has been collected, it's time to analyze it and summarize it. Don't spend too much time on Step 4. Glaring problems usually emerge without doing lots of calculations. Little is gained by continually refining calculations.

If time data has been collected, you should calculate work efficiency and process cycle time. You also might want to calculate associated labor costs. Once again, calculate and summarize what makes sense.

A data summary chart is an effective tool for illustrating collected data. By presenting all collected data in a data summary chart, areas for improvement usually become obvious.

A data summary chart for the assemble-widget process is illustrated in Figure 5.4.

Step		Steps	Minutes
Operation	○	3	10
Transportation	▶	7	15
Delay	D	3	3
Inspection	□	1	2
Storage	▽		
Rework	®		
Total		14	30

Figure 5.4 The data summary chart.

Sometimes, a simple bar graph is also very effective for summarizing data. Based on our assemble-widget data summary chart, a bar graph displaying the percentage of total cycle time for each process step type is illustrated in Figure 5.5.

66 | *The Process Reengineering Workbook*

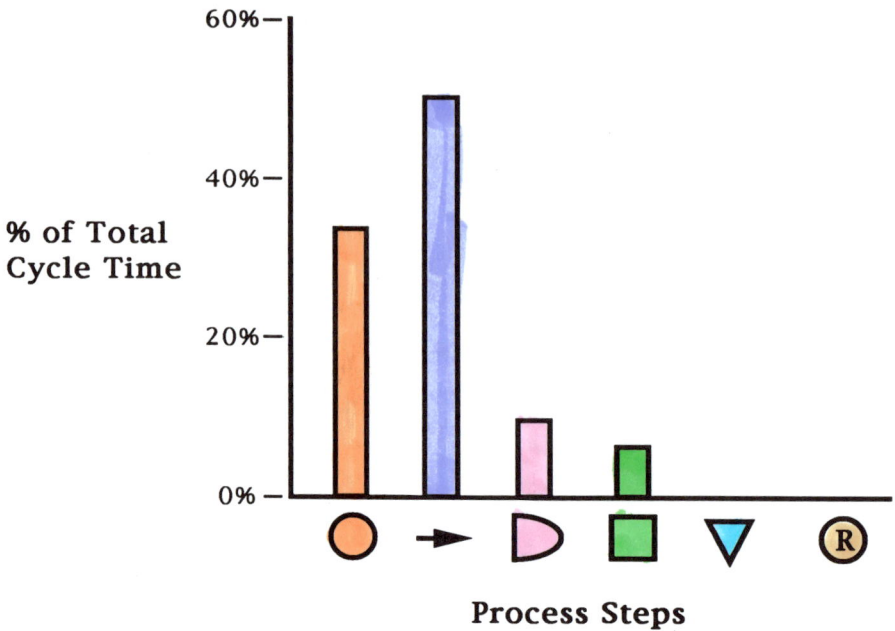

Figure 5.5

At the end of Step 4, all process-related data is analyzed (but not to death!), summarized, and illustrated in an appropriate format. At the end of Step 4, you have:

- Summarized all metrics for each process step.
- Completed a data summary chart.

Step 5. Identify improvement areas. If you've done Steps 1 through 4 correctly, Step 5 can be relatively easy. Your improvement targets should be obvious. Because the goal of process reengineering is eliminating or minimizing waste, your first targets should always be transportation, delay, inspection, rework, and storage. When these steps have been eliminated or minimized, you can begin improving operation steps.

Good candidates to target for improvement include:

- Redundant or unnecessary transportation steps.
- Time-consuming transportation steps.
- Redundant or unnecessary delay steps.
- Time-consuming delay steps.
- Redundant inspection steps.
- All rework steps.
- Inefficient process layouts.
- Inefficient process sequences or flows.

When looking for areas to improve, you should ask such questions as:

- What is the purpose or function of this step?
- Does this step directly add value to the process?
- Can the step be eliminated? If it is eliminated, what is the effect on the quality and reliability of the output?
- If the step cannot be eliminated, can it be minimized?
- Can the step be combined with an operation step?

Step 5 should take very little time. At the end of Step 5, specific improvement targets are identified. Improvements are also prioritized—that is, you should have a good idea of what needs to be improved first, second, and so on.

Remember, improvement priorities are based on quantitative data, not opinions or an "I think so." That's the beauty of the seven-step PI method. It's systematic, it's defensible, it's quantifiable, and it's fact-based. Management likes that.

When Step 5 is complete, improvement areas are identified and prioritized. Armed with this information, we can start the improvement portion of process reengineering. That's what Step 6 is all about. Once again, after Step 5, you have:

- Identified potential improvement areas.
- Prioritized improvement areas.

Step 6. Develop improvements. Step 6 involves actually designing and developing a process improvement. It's the cure for the identified ailment. Chapter 6 discusses process improvement ideas in detail. Process improvement ideas to consider include:

- Eliminating various process steps, especially non-value adding steps.
- Minimizing the time associated with certain steps.
- Reducing process complexity by simplifying the process.
- Selecting an alternative transportation method.
- Combining various process steps.
- Changing a linear process into a parallel process.
- Using decision-based, alternative process paths.
- Changing the sequence of process steps.
- Using technology to increase process effectiveness or efficiency.
- Letting customers do some of the process work.

The engineering phrase "eliminate, simplify, and combine" is good advice. So is KISS, which stands for keep it simple stupid! Simple, inexpensive improvements can translate into huge savings in quality, cycle time, and costs.

In selecting a process improvement, make sure that the cure doesn't cost more than the illness. This is especially true if expensive, high-tech equipment is to be purchased. A cost-benefit analysis may be necessary. If so, get help from the accounting department.

68 | *The Process Reengineering Workbook*

A Before-After chart is an effective method for documenting expected gains from a proposed improvement. It compares the process before and after the proposed improvement. A blank Before-After chart using time as a metric is shown in Figure 5.6.

	Before		After	
Step	Steps	Minutes	Steps	Minutes
Operation ○				
Transportation ➤				
Delay ▷				
Inspection □				
Storage ▽				
Rework Ⓡ				
Total				

Figure 5.6

Let's consider an example using a Before-After chart. Remember the assemble-widget process? Transportation is an obvious improvement target. It accounts for approximately 50 percent of total process cycle time. Looking at the process overhead view diagram, most of the transportation steps are associated with walking back and forth to the parts bin (see Figure 5.7).

One improvement might involve changing the location of the parts bins—that is, changing the process layout. Instead of placing them in a separate room, the parts bins could be directly above the widget assembly bench. This eliminates all transportation steps.

Instead of two general ones, you might also want to have separate bins for widget legs, arms, and heads. By separating the bins, you can reduce the delay associated with looking for the right part. After reengineering the physical layout of the process, a Before-After chart might look like the example in Figure 5.8.

By rearranging the physical layout, we've reduced cycle time by 16.5 minutes. We've also improved work efficiency from 33 percent to 75 percent. Not too bad!

Step 6 of the seven-step PI method, involves developing an appropriate improvement. It also includes calculating expected gains. After Step 6, you have:

- Developed specific improvements.
- Calculated potential gains.
- Completed before-after comparisons.

The Seven-Step PI Method | 69

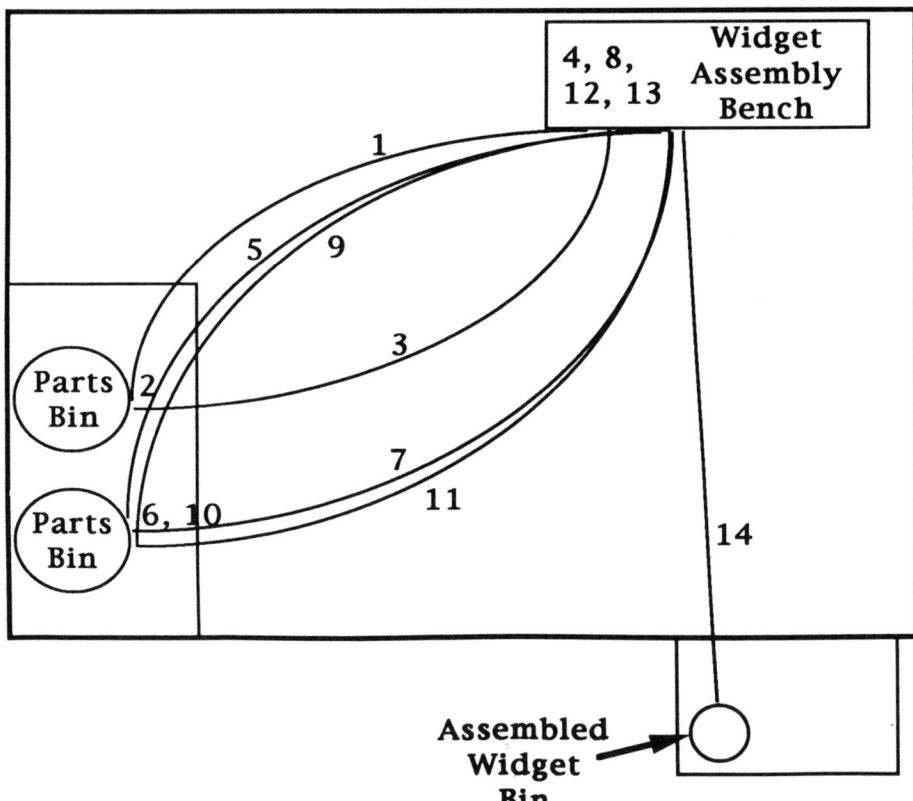

Figure 5.7 Process overhead view diagram.

Step	Before		After	
	Steps	Minutes	Steps	Minutes
Operation ○	3	10	3	10
Transportation ➤	7	15		
Delay ▷	3	3	3	1.5
Inspection ☐	1	2	1	2
Storage ▽				
Rework Ⓡ				
Total	14	30	7	13.5

Figure 5.8

Step 7. Implement and monitor improvements. Step 7 involves implementing the developed improvement. This is the putting-it-to-work step. Process improvements are commonly implemented in one of three ways:

- A pilot run.
- A complete switch over.
- A gradual phase in.

A *pilot run* is like a test. You try it and see if it is going to work. A *complete switch over* is just doing it. One minute it's the old way, the next minute it's the new way. A *gradual phase in* is a graded transition to the improvement.

Which way is best? It depends on several facts. It depends on the cost of the improvement. It also depends on the complexity and associated risk of failure. A complete switch over is appropriate for simple process improvements that can be easily implemented and with little risk of failure. Complex or high-tech processes typically require the pilot route. Gradual phase in makes sense for process improvements that carry high costs for failure. Once again, the correct implementation method depends on the cost, complexity, and chance of failure.

Whenever a new process improvement has been implemented, it must be monitored. In Step 6, a proposed Before-After chart was created. In Step 7, a real one can be developed. Both charts should be similar. If not, try to figure out why and take corrective actions. A word of caution: Don't always expect huge miracles at the beginning. Sometimes, a short adjustment period is required.

Step 7 consists of implementing the developed improvement. It's the let's-see-if-this-actually-works step. Once an improvement is implemented, it also must be monitored. After Step 7, you have:

- Identified the implementation method.
- Implemented the improvement method.
- Monitored the improvement.

Summary of the Seven-Step PI Method

To review, the seven-step PI method consists of:

1. Defining process boundaries.
2. Observing process steps.
3. Collecting process-related data.
4. Analyzing collected data.
5. Identifying improvement areas.
6. Developing improvements.
7. Implementing and monitoring improvements.

The seven-step PI method is simple and easy to use, but it is also very powerful. By systematically following the seven-step PI method, companies can significantly improve their work processes.

Don't forget, the goal of process reengineering is to make significant improvements. Although it's not just analysis, some analysis is required. It's hard to fix something if we don't know what needs fixing. That's why we need to collect metrics, or quantitative data. Metrics allow us to make improvements based on fact, not opinion.

Let's look at two examples of the seven-step PI method in action. The two examples were introduced in Chapter 4. In this chapter, we'll apply the seven-step PI method. In Chapter 7, it's your turn to do some process reengineering.

Example 1

Our first example deals with the field engineers from Chapter 4. Their job is to maintain and repair complex hospital imaging and X-ray equipment. One problem they face is having to make repeated trips to their service vans to retrieve information. Let's see if we can't improve this process a bit.

Step 1. Define process boundaries. The repair-and-maintain-imaging-equipment process is chosen. We'll call it the service process for short. The process begins with the field engineer reaching the job site. It ends with repaired and maintained equipment. The output is a service. The purpose of the process analysis is to improve efficiency by shortening process cycle time. Time is chosen as a metric. Because the focus of the analysis is on a human doing something, a process task analysis is performed. Before beginning Step 2, you receive a short overview of the service process.

Step 2. Observe process steps. You accompany several field engineers to the job site, and you observe the service process. You record your observations using a process analysis worksheet. On the worksheet, you record:

- A short description of each step.
- The proper step sequence.
- The flow and type of each step.

A typical process analysis worksheet is shown in Figure 5.9.

As you record your observations and descriptions, you realize that the four repair imaging equipment steps (1, 5, 9, and 13) actually are an activity that can be subdivided into a series of process steps. For the purpose of this analysis, however, little would be gained from the extra work. You decide to leave the repair imaging equipment steps as they are.

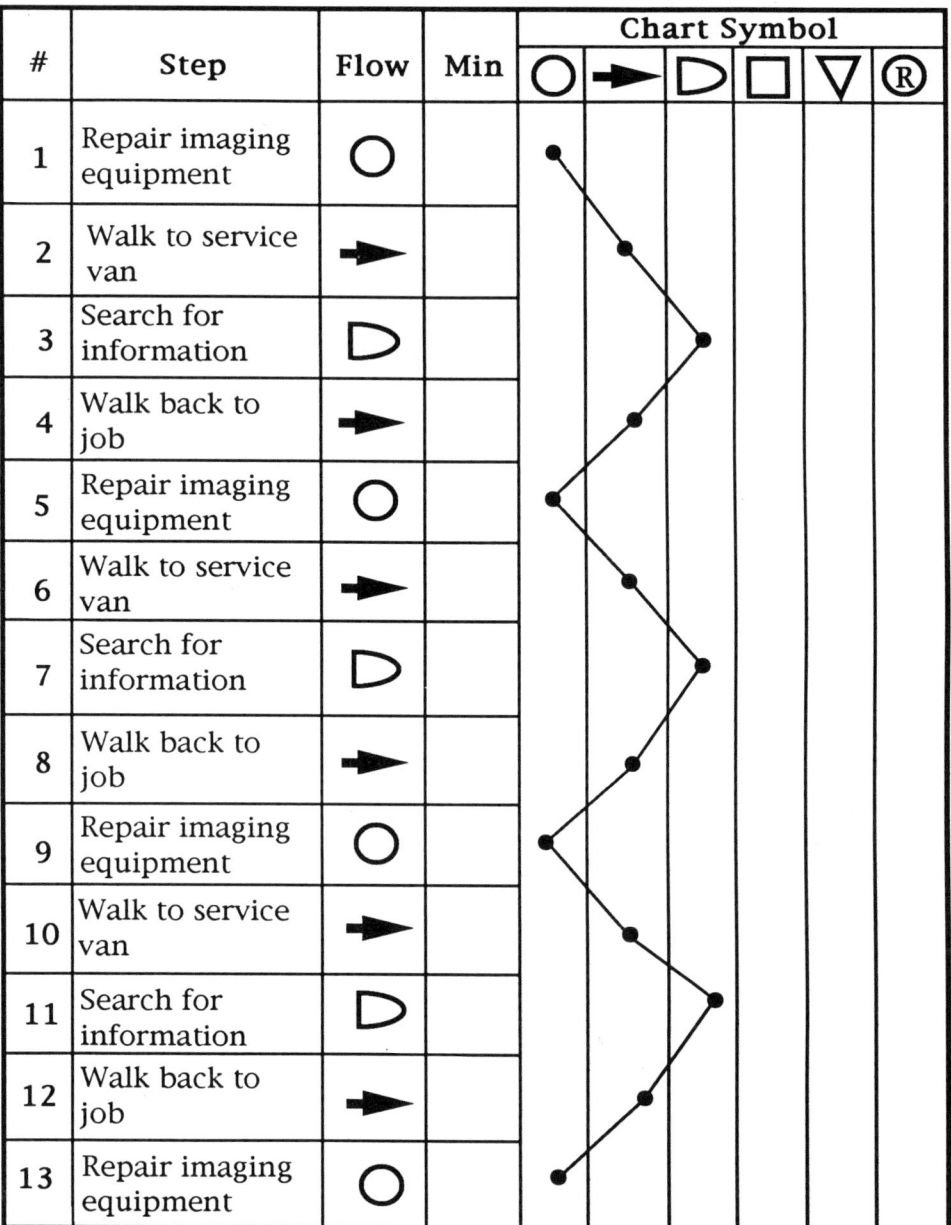

Figure 5.9 Process task analysis worksheet: repair equipment.

Step 3. Collect process-related data. While observing the process during Step 2, you also collect time data. You fill in the appropriate Min (minutes) column of the process analysis worksheet (see Figure 5.10).

#	STEP	FLOW	MIN	Chart Symbol ○ → ▷ □ ▽ ®
1	Repair imaging equipment	○	90	
2	Walk to service van	→	12	
3	Search for information	▷	6	
4	Walk back to job	→	12	
5	Repair imaging equipment	○	75	
6	Walk to service van	→	12	
7	Search for information	▷	6	
8	Walk back to job	→	12	
9	Repair imaging equipment	○	80	
10	Walk to service van	→	12	
11	Search for information	▷	6	
12	Walk back to job	→	12	
13	Repair imaging equipment	○	25	

Figure 5.10 Process task analysis worksheet: repair equipment

Step 4. Analyze collected data. From the data collected in Steps 2 and 3, you develop a data summary chart (see Figure 5.11).

Step		Steps	Minutes
Operation	◯	4	270
Transportation	▶	6	72
Delay	D	3	18
Inspection	☐		
Storage	▽		
Rework	Ⓡ		
Total		13	360

Figure 5.11 The completed data summary chart.

From the data summary chart, you calculate work efficiency. Work efficiency is:

$$\text{Work Efficiency} = \frac{270}{270 + 90} \times 100\% = 75\%$$

To better illustrate the summarized data, you also develop a bar chart, as illustrated in Figure 5.12.

Step 5. Identify improvement areas. The summarized data suggests that transportation is a good candidate for initial improvement. Reviewing the process analysis worksheets, you note that all of the transportation steps are associated with going back and forth to the van to look up needed information. You target getting information for improvement. Using information adds value, getting it doesn't.

Step 6. Develop improvements. Reviewing the collected information, you realize that you need to eliminate all transportation steps and still provide the needed information. Your first thought is to have the field engineers carry all of the manuals, procedures, schematics, and other documentation to the job site. However, several trips would be necessary because these materials weigh approximately 150 pounds. This really won't save anything, so you decide to look for other solutions.

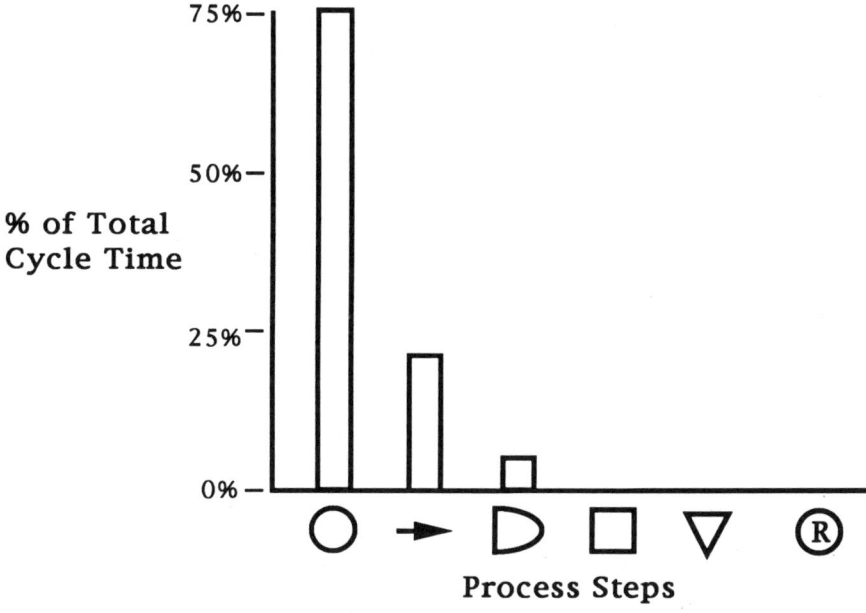

Figure 5.12

You consider storing all of the material on a small notebook computer. That way, the field engineers have to carry only the notebook computer to the job site. This eliminates all transportation steps. It will also probably reduce delay times associated with searching for information. You do a quick Before-After chart, in which you eliminate all transportation times and cut delay times in half (see Figure 5.13).

Step	Before		After	
	Steps	Minutes	Steps	Minutes
Operation ○	4	270	4	270
Transportation ➤	6	72		
Delay ⌓	3	18	3	9
Inspection □				
Storage ▽				
Rework ⓡ				
Total	13	360	7	279

Figure 5.13

By implementing this improvement, work efficiency increases from 75 percent to 97 percent (270/270 + 9). However, you realize that purchasing notebook computers and formatting the data for all 750 field engineers is an expensive undertaking. Before suggesting such an investment, you quickly calculate potential savings.

Based on your proposed Before-After chart, you will save approximately 81 minutes per job (360 − 279 = 81).

$$81 \text{ minutes}/60 \text{ minutes} = 1.35 \text{ hours}$$

$$1.35 \text{ hours} \times \$50/\text{labor hour} = \$67.50 \text{ savings per job}$$

Multiplying $67.50 times 208 working days per year times the number of engineers (i.e., 750) gives you a potential savings of:

$$\$67.50 \times 208 \times 750 = \$10,530,000$$

However, this calculated number, isn't quite right. You will not be able to realize the entire $10.53 million in savings. Although field engineers perform multiple jobs at the same site, they still must move from site to site. You figure that only about 2/3 of the time will they be able to realize the potential savings. Therefore:

$$\$10,530,000 \times .66 = \$6,949,800$$

Such potential savings still justify buying notebook computers.

Step 7. Implement and monitor improvements. You present your findings to management. They are impressed with the thoroughness of your analysis and with the potential cost savings. Although they question the idea that computers can solve all problems, they can't dismiss your analysis. It is agreed that a pilot project should be undertaken. A select group of field engineers will be given fully loaded notebook computers. They will also receive any needed training. You are instructed to implement the program and monitor its status for six months. Then, you are to report back with the results.

Six months later you return. The pilot project has been a huge success. The field engineers using the computers can't imagine working without them. Cost savings, when translated into productivity gains, have been very impressive. After the pilot program, you are able to refine expected savings. You suggest that in the first year, the company will achieve approximately $4 million in productivity gains. Your projections include costs of purchasing computers, loading needed information, training, and so on. For the following year, you predict approximately $7 million in productivity gains.

Example 2

Our second example deals with the large company, described in Chapter 4, that is experiencing problems in processing requisition forms. It seems to take forever to get supplies and materials ordered and delivered to a worksite.

Step 1. Define process boundaries. The requisition process is targeted for improvement. However, because of the size of the process, you decide to divide it into three smaller, more manageable subprocesses:

- Requisition form completion and authorization (req for short).
- Ordering.
- Receiving and delivery.

Your assignment is to improve the req subprocess. This subprocess begins with initiating a requisition form. It ends with the completed and approved form being mailed to ordering. The output is a completed and approved requisition form. The purpose of the process analysis is to improve efficiency by shortening cycle time. Time is the chosen metric. Because the focus of the analysis is on an object (i.e., a completed form), a process product analysis is conducted. Before beginning Step 2, you receive a short overview of the subprocess. Interestingly, everyone thinks a particular individual is responsible for the extensive delays.

Step 2. Observe process steps. First, you develop a traveler to accompany a dozen requisition forms. The traveler is illustrated in Figure 5.14. You brief all involved personnel before sending out the traveler. The briefing includes the purpose of the study as well the types of steps to record. For example, few people would think of a form sitting in an in basket as a process step.

Process Traveler				
Date	Time In	Time Out	Description	Initials

Figure 5.14

After the requisition forms are completed and approved, you retrieve the travelers. From the completed travelers, you are able to develop a representative process analysis worksheet for the req subprocess. It's shown in Figure 5.15.

#	Step	Flow	Min	○	→	D	□	▽	®
1	Requisition form initiated	○		●					
2	Form mailed to Procurement	→			●				
3	Form sits in in basket	D				●			
4	Requisition form completed	○		●					
5	Form sits in out basket	D				●			
6	Form mailed to Authorization	→			●				
7	Form sits in in basket	D				●			
8	Form reviewed & authorized	□					●		
9	Form sits in out basket	D				●			
10	Form mailed to Ordering	→			●				

Figure 5.15 Process product analysis worksheet: requisition form.

Step 3. Collect process-related data. From the completed travelers, you also record all process step times. You then develop a representative process analysis worksheet, complete with average times (see Figure 5.16).

#	Step	Flow	Min	Chart Symbol ○	→	▷	□	▽	ⓡ
1	Requisition form initiated	○	10	●					
2	Form mailed to Procurement	→	720		●				
3	Form sits in in basket	▷	75			●			
4	Requisition form completed	○	18	●					
5	Form sits in out basket	▷	75			●			
6	Form mailed to Authorization	→	720		●				
7	Form sits in in basket	▷	45			●			
8	Form reviewed & authorized	□	12				●		
9	Form sits in out basket	▷	90			●			
10	Form mailed to Ordering	→	720		●				

Figure 5.16 Process product analysis worksheet: requisition form.

Step 4. Analyze collected data. With the completed process analysis worksheets, you develop a data summary chart (see Figure 5.17).

Step		Steps	Minutes
Operation	○	2	28
Transportation	▶	3	2160
Delay	◁	4	275
Inspection	□	1	12
Storage	▽		
Rework	Ⓡ		
Total		10	2475

Figure 5.17 The data summary chart.

You also create a bar graph of the summarized findings (see Figure 5.18).

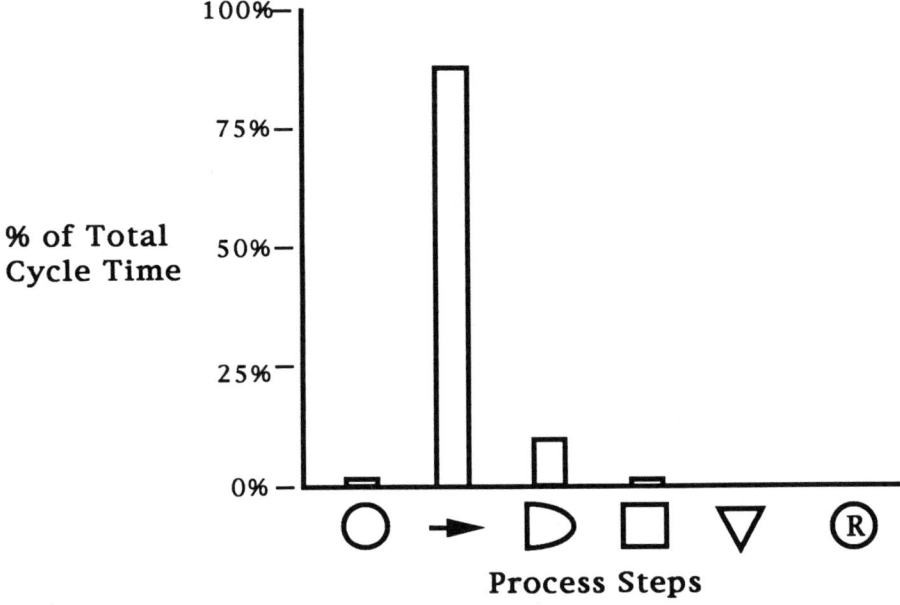

Figure 5.18

You also calculate work efficiency. Work efficiency for the req subprocess is 1 percent:

$$\text{Work Efficiency} = \frac{28}{28 + 2447} \times 100\% = 1\%$$

Step 5. Identify improvement areas. From the collected data, it is obvious that the req subprocess needs major improvement. Eliminating all transportation steps is an obvious place to start. Sending the forms through the mail simply takes too long!

Step 6. Develop improvements. Because transportation accounts for 87 percent of total cycle time, you begin to think of alternative transportation methods. Using fax machines to transport the forms is an obvious answer, because every office seems to have one.

You also take a second look at the process flow, which looks like this:

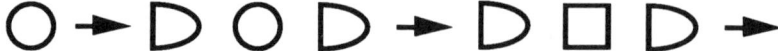

You question the need for the second operation step. Why does one person initiate the form and another person complete the form? Why doesn't the first person do both? When you ask these questions, no one really knows. The most common reply is, "That's the way it's always been done." You eliminate the second person completing the form. The first person now initiates and completes the form.

The inspection step near the end of the subprocess is a review and authorization step, but that review and authorization step is needed for only the small portion of the requisition forms that exceed a certain dollar amount. The rest of the forms don't require review and authorization.

When you ask why all forms are sent for review and authorization, you are told that this ensures that "those forms that need approval are approved!" This is a classic example of designing a process for the exception, even if that exception rarely happens.

You redesign the process to include a decision branch. If the requisition form exceeds a certain dollar amount, it is faxed for review and authorization. If it doesn't exceed that amount, it is faxed directly to Ordering. The redesigned req subprocess now looks like this:

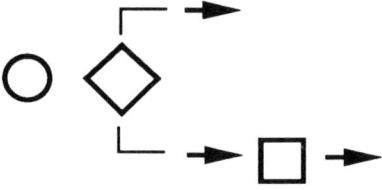

Note the extensive changes from the old process, which looked like this:

O D → D O D → D □ D →

Following the seven-step PI method, you have eliminated sending the forms through the company mail. They're now faxed. You've also eliminated a second operation step by combining two operations into a single step. You've also eliminated the inspection step except for those cases when it is really needed.

You complete a Before-After chart for the majority of cases (i.e., those that don't require approval). Your reengineering efforts have reduced cycle time from 2,475 minutes to 24 minutes, a savings of 2,451 minutes or almost 41 hours (see Figure 5.19). Work efficiency has also increased from 1% to 83%—not a bad day of process reengineering!

Step	Before Steps	Before Minutes	After Steps	After Minutes
Operation ○	2	28	1	20
Transportation ➤	3	2160	1	4
Delay D	4	275		
Inspection □	1	12		
Storage ▽				
Rework ⓡ				
Total	10	2475	2	24

Figure 5.19

Step 7. Implement and monitor improvements. You present your findings to management. They are very enthusiastic about your suggested improvements. No additional expenses are associated with the improvement. There is also little risk of failure. As a result, you implement a complete switch over to the newly redesigned req subprocess. Subsequent monitoring of the reengineered process reveals no problems. In fact, it works just fine.

Summary

Efforts to improve processes must be fact-based. That is, process improvements should be based on the systematic observation and collection of quantitative data. This allows us to focus on major problems first. It also allows us to eliminate huge amounts of waste up front.

The seven-step PI method helps us ensure that we conduct process reengineering efforts in a systematic manner. The seven process improvement steps are:

1. Define process boundaries.
2. Observe process steps.
3. Collect process-related data.
4. Analyze collected data.
5. Identify improvement areas.
6. Develop improvements.
7. Implement and monitor improvements.

By following these seven steps, we can significantly improve our work processes. We can make them better, faster, and cheaper. Such efforts can also make our work easier, less fatiguing, and hopefully, more enjoyable.

Process Improvement Principles

Although there are many ways to improve processes, the basic theme is always the same: eliminate or minimize waste. Remember, waste adds only delay and cost, which companies can ill afford in today's highly competitive business world.

In this chapter, we'll present nine process improvement principles. This is a good start. If applied properly, these basic principles can greatly improve any process. With time, you'll want to add to this basic list. But for now, let's just concentrate on the nine. The nine principles are:

1. Eliminate waste.
2. Minimize waste.
3. Simplify, simplify, simplify.
4. Whenever possible, combine process steps.
5. Design processes with alternative paths.
6. Think parallel, not linear.
7. Collect data once at its source.
8. Use technology to improve processes.
9. Let customers assist in the process.

Let's examine each of these principles in greater detail.

Principle 1: Eliminate waste. The golden rule of process reengineering is eliminate waste. Waste is bad. Waste results in long cycle times, poor work efficiencies, and added costs.

Most processes contain lots of waste, including delay, transportation, inspection, rework, and storage steps. Whenever possible, eliminate these steps:

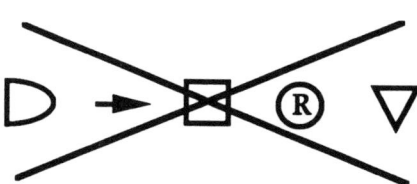

How do we eliminate waste? By learning to spot waste sequences. You need to recognize clumps of waste-adding process steps, such as a delay-transportation-delay sequence:

Other waste sequence to watch out for include rework sequences, repeated transportation and storage sequences, and multiple inspections.

In addition, you should always identify the real purpose of any process. You need to identify the desired output, then determine what happens to that output if certain process steps are eliminated. If nothing bad happens, the steps are likely candidates for elimination.

Let's look at an example. The Have Flower Will Travel Company is in the flower business. It specializes in getting freshly picked flowers to market as fast as possible.

Their process for getting to the market as fast as possible is illustrated in Figure 6.1. However, it's really not very fast. It's actually quite slow. Why? Because it includes unnecessary and redundant storage and transportation steps that extend cycle time. These steps make the process slower, not faster.

The process is reengineered. All intermediate storage and transportation steps are eliminated. These steps don't directly add value to the output: delivered flowers. The new, reengineered process is shown to the right of the old one. It now consists of only three steps. No longer are the flowers stored at intermediate storage facilities. Instead, they're transported directly to market.

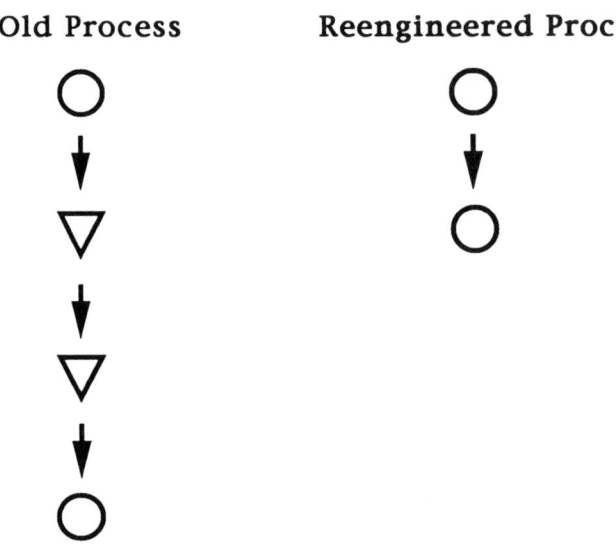

Figure 6.1

Principle 2: Minimize waste. Sometimes waste can't be eliminated. When it can't be eliminated, we need to at least minimize it.

For example, sending a company form from one person to another usually involves a wasteful delay-transportation-delay sequence in which the form moves from an out basket through company mail to an in basket:

Let's assume that in this case, transportation is by company mail. We may not be able to eliminate this transportation step, but we can certainly minimize it. That is, we can minimize the time associated with the transportation step, mailing form. We can fax the form instead of mailing it. This minimizes transportation time. Transportation time isn't eliminated but it is certainly minimized it. However, faxing does eliminate one delay step. The new process sequence now looks like this:

Selecting a different transportation method often reduces cycle time. The company mail might take 24 hours. A fax takes only a few minutes. In this example, the fax machine represents a transportation minimization device, or TMD (see Figure 6.2).

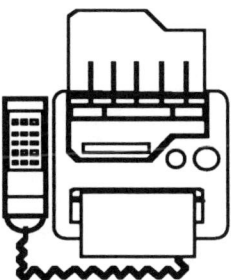

Figure 6.2 Fax as TMD.

Let's look at another example. An engineer is working on a design project. The engineer needs the weight of 2-inch standard metal pipe to enter into an equation. To get the needed information, the engineer:

1. Walks to a bookcase (transportation).
2. Searches for the right manual (delay).
3. Finds the manual and carries it back to the desk (transportation).
4. Searches through the manual for the correct weight (delay).
5. Finds the weight and enters it into an equation (operation).
6. Returns the manual to the bookcase (transportation).

88 | *The Process Reengineering Workbook*

This process sequence is repeated several times a day. It consumes approximately 20 percent of each engineer's day.

The getting information process sequence contains lots of waste. A flowchart of this process sequence looks like this:

Ideally, we would eliminate the getting-information sequence altogether. Unfortunately, we can't. Engineers need lots of information to plug into all kinds of equations. That's part of being an engineer. If we can't eliminate it, however, we can usually minimize it. Let's see how.

All the engineers in the company have computers. Why not use these for the getting-information sequence? A data base containing frequently used information is created. The data base is then loaded into each engineer's computer. Now, instead of getting information manually, information is retrieved via the computer. The new getting-information sequence looks like this:

Engineers no longer need to constantly get up from their desks and search through bulky manuals. Now all they have to do is press a few buttons on a keyboard. In this example, the computer is a delay minimization device or DMD (see Figure 6.3).

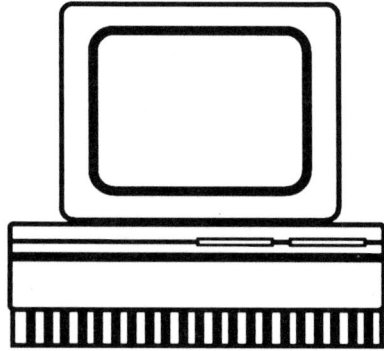

Figure 6.3 Computer as DMD.

We not only minimized waste in this example, we also eliminated it. By minimizing the getting-information sequence, we eliminated:

- Three transportation steps.
- One delay step.

When we set out to minimize waste, we often end up eliminating some waste as well. In other words, we combine principle 1 and principle 2.

You might argue that in the engineering example, the computer is nothing but a fast page turner, and not a marvelous, high-tech solution. You're right, and you'll get no argument! However, that fast page turner helped us significantly reduce cycle time, and time is money. Principle 8 also applies here. It relates to using technology to eliminate and minimize waste.

So, principle 2 is all about minimizing waste. If you can't eliminate it, minimize it.

Principle 3: Simplify, simplify, simplify. Processes should be as simple as possible. Simple processes contain a minimal number of process steps. Simple processes also have steps that are easy to understand and easy to execute. We like processes that contain understandable and executable steps.

Simple processes are good. They have short cycle times, they have low costs, and they produce fewer defects.

Unfortunately, most of our processes aren't simple. Instead, they're complex. When we map out our processes, they contain lots of steps. They resemble the following process:

Because there are so many steps, we usually have a hard time understanding complex processes. We also have a hard time executing all of those process steps.

Because they contain lots of steps, complex processes also have long cycle times. Long cycle times mean high costs. Complex processes are also susceptible to high rates of defects. With more steps, there's simply a higher probability of making more mistakes. Therefore, complex processes aren't better, faster, or cheaper. In fact, they're just the opposite.

How do processes become complex? Sometimes we purposely design them that way. We think that the more little boxes there are on a process flowchart, the better the process. Or we think that mazes of boxes going all directions look very impressive. We start to believe these complex process designs are something we can show off to management.

Guided by these false beliefs, we add lots of steps. We think more is better, but that belief is false! More is not better. More is not impressive. More only adds delay, cost, and a high probability of failure. Fewer is better. Fewer is impressive. Fewer is faster, better, and cheaper. Always go for fewer, not for more.

Processes also become more complex over time. They simply grow or evolve that way. They grow from being fairly simple to very complex. Why? Because, instead of constantly eliminating steps (principle 1), we always add steps. We never eliminate. We just add, and add, and add.

Adding steps increases process complexity. Adding steps is not good. For example, as shown in Figure 6.4, we might start with a simple process (Time 1). In this case, the process has only three steps. Then something happens. We turn out a defective product and management panics. Management wants immediate action. The solution? We add an inspection step (Time 2). We discover the defect and that's the end of the problem—or so we think.

Then something else happens. Same panic, same demand for action, same answer: add another inspection step (Time 3). By the time we do all of this adding, our process has changed. It has grown. It has become more complex.

The problem with this idea of adding a step is that we never add just one step. Instead, we almost always add several steps. We often create three or four additional steps for every one that we think we're adding. We add one, and we get two, three, or four extra. What a deal!

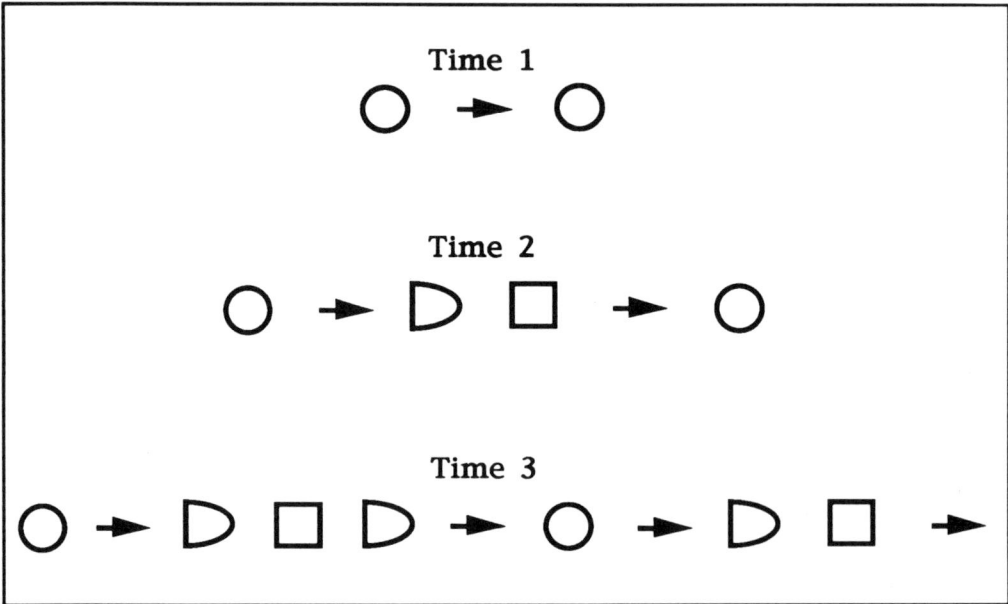

Figure 6.4 Processes commonly grow with time.

For example, we might want to add just one additional review (inspection) step:

However, adding this single step usually requires adding other steps as well—for example, like additional transportation and delay steps. The single inspection step is now flanked by transportation and delay steps:

It's these hidden transportation and delay steps that we never think about that allow processes to grow at such alarming rates. One step mysteriously grows into five steps. It takes only a few such growth spurts to greatly increase process complexity, and with that increased complexity come such problems as longer cycle times, higher costs, and greater risk of error.

If a process is experiencing a problem, fix the problem. Don't simply add more steps. Adding an inspection step is not going to fix anything. An inspection step can only detect a problem, it can't fix anything. We'll talk more about inspection steps in principle 4.

Adding steps also frequently increases the number of people involved in the process. More people often means more organizations. More people and more organizations translate into big problems, including breakdowns in communication, coordination, and ownership.

To eliminate or minimize all of these problems, we want to keep processes as simple as possible. Simple processes contain a minimal number of steps, a minimal number of people, and a minimal number of organizations. Minimal is good.

One way to minimize all of this is to pack as much work as possible into each operation step. Each step should be designed to accomplish as much work as possible before that work is handed off to someone else.

Always follow principle 3. Practice the philosophy of KISS. Keep processes simple. If you do, everything works better, life is happier, and life is much less complicated.

Principle 4: Whenever possible, combine process steps. As noted, you can't always eliminate waste. Sometimes you're stuck with it. When this happens, think of ways to combine the waste step with a work step. That way, you can add value even when you're not adding value!

You combine process steps all the time at home. For example, you might call someone from a portable phone to ask for information and get one of those messages that tells you, "the next available agent will be with you as soon as possible." Rather than simply standing there waiting, you walk to the kitchen and empty the dishwasher. In this example, you have combined a delay step (i.e., waiting on hold) with an operation step (i.e., emptying the dishwasher). We need to do more of this combining at work.

Combining operation and inspection steps is a good place to start. A typical process flow might look like this example:

Note the two inspection steps and all of the delay and transportation steps associated with these two steps. An inspection step is really a package deal, but this package deal contains lots of waste. In other words, it's a package deal we really don't want.

Let's examine inspection steps. The following diagram shows a successful inspection sequence in which a product goes to QA and passes inspection:

In this sequence, the product:

○ → ▷ □ → ▽

- Is assembled.
- Is transported to an inspection site.
- Waits for the inspection.
- Passes the inspection.
- Is transported to storage.
- Is stored before being shipped to market.

However, a failed inspection usually means:

- Some rework is required.
- An additional inspection step is needed.

The following diagram shows a failed inspection sequence:

As illustrated, failed inspections add lots of delay and cost to any process.

In the preceding example, everything after the first operational step is simply waste. This includes both inspection steps. All those steps must be completed, but not one of them is adding value or directly moving the process forward. This is not good! But how can we improve it?

First, it's important to understand what an inspection is and what it isn't. An inspection can only detect a defect. It can't fix it. Rework fixes defects. Inspections only detect them. Wouldn't it be nice if we could fix a defect when it happens rather than several process steps later?

Detecting and correcting errors at their source eliminates the need for subsequent inspection and rework steps. Remember, inspection and rework steps are usually package deals that also contain numerous transportation and delay steps.

Combining an inspection step and an operation step is often an effective way to detect and correct errors at their source. This has several benefits. It eliminates individual inspection and rework steps. It also eliminates transportation and delay associated with these steps. If we combine operations and inspections, our reengineered process for a failed inspection changes from this:

to this:

Look at the savings. By combining steps, we eliminate lots of waste. We've reduced the number of process steps for a rework example from 11 to only 3.

Inspection and operation steps can be combined in many ways. For example, one company found that its employees were filling out forms incorrectly. The forms were very important legal documents that were submitted monthly to a government agency, so they had to be filled out exactly right.

Unfortunately, the company was experiencing a defect rate of approximately 30 percent. When an error was detected, the person committing the error had to be located by a quality control person. Then the problem had to be fixed. Correcting the errors was costing the company approximately $1 million dollars annually. Although the company had added multiple inspections, they hadn't done anything to eliminate the problem at its source. They were only detecting errors, not preventing them.

Realizing the magnitude of the problem, they adopted a prevent it, don't inspect it philosophy. Examining the problem, they found that most of the mistakes were quite simple—for example, some employees used their signatures instead of printing their names. Others forgot to specify whether the time they entered was AM or PM.

Management's first thought was to fix the *who*. They considered offering training to all of those employees responsible for filling out forms, but then they remembered that the people had been trained. Then they looked at the *what*. They examined the form.

The old form is shown in Figure 6.5.

Name:

Time:

Date:

Figure 6.5

Do you see anything wrong with it? The form doesn't provide any cues or hints on how to fill it out correctly. It doesn't allow people to inspect their own work or determine whether their input is correct.

The company solved the problem by redesigning the form. The new form makes it possible for people to inspect their own work. The new form is shown in Figure 6.6.

The new form contains plenty of cues to help users determine if it is being filled out properly. The results of the redesign effort? The 30 percent defect rate has been eliminated. In addition, independent inspections and costly rework steps

94 | *The Process Reengineering Workbook*

```
Print Name: _____
                 Last              First            MI


Time: _____   ☐ AM
       Check Box  ☐ PM


Date:  ___/___/___
       MO  DA  YR
```

Figure 6.6

are no longer needed. The fix was simple (KISS), yet it saved the company $1 million in inspections and rework.

So whenever possible, think of ways to combine inspection and operation steps. Think smart. Get creative. Ask yourself, "How do I know if I've done this correctly?" If I don't know, provide information so that I do know.

Also, think of ways to prevent someone from making a mistake. Try to determine whether it is possible to make a step mistake proof. For example, if a part can be inserted right side up or upside down, redesign the part. Design it so it can be inserted only one way, the right way.

Other process step combinations can also prove effective. For example, we can't always avoid delays. In such cases try to combine the delay step with an operation step, or combine a transportation step with an operation step. If you're transporting something, can you work on it at the same time? Sometimes you can, sometimes you can't. However, you should always think in terms of combinations. Combinations are good.

One final thought on combining steps: Don't ignore the possibility of combining two or more operational steps. Two operational steps frequently represent at least three process steps. By combining two operational steps, we can streamline the process from this:

to this:

Always try to make each operational step as full of work as possible. Don't pass on operational steps prematurely. Make them count for as much as possible. That's good reengineering.

Think combinations. That's what principle 4 is all about.

Principle 5: Design processes with alternative paths. Most processes are designed for the exception, not the rule. Although such processes catch the exception, they carry a high price in terms of process efficiency and cost. However, some exceptions are real, and you will encounter cases when it makes sense to add reviews and authorizations.

The question we must ask is: Do we design for the exception or the rule? The answer is that we design for both—the exception and the rule. Now, however, there is no exception or rule. Instead, there are alternatives—alternative process routes.

Remember decision points?

Decision Point

A decision point is similar to an IF...THEN...statement. IF this is true, THEN do something. IF this is false, THEN do something else. For example, a decision point in a process might be:

IF invoice is greater than $10,000, THEN select process path 1.
IF invoice is less than $10,000, THEN select process path 2.

Another example might be:

IF applicant has good credit rating, THEN select process path 1.
IF applicant has bad credit rating, THEN select process path 2.

Get the picture? By using decision points, we can eliminate lots of unnecessary process steps that represent waste.

For example, one company processed all life insurance applications the same way. The claims went through the same process sequence whether the applicant was a high risk or a low risk. Unfortunately, that process sequence was very time consuming. It also involved several people handling the same application. The process looked like this:

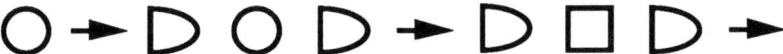

As you can see, the process contains numerous steps. Several of these steps are needed for high-risk individuals. The company can lose considerable money on these folks, so the company must be cautious.

However, all the steps aren't necessary for low-risk individuals. These low-risk folks form the bulk of the applicants.

The reengineering solution involves adding a decision point to the process. The new process now looks like this:

After some initial work on the application (the first operational step), a few decision questions are asked. If the questions are answered one way, the application is automatically approved and sent directly to billing. Just a quick look and approval, then the application goes straight to billing. This direct route is represented by the top path.

If the questions are answered another way, the lower path is chosen. This path takes considerably longer because it requires an additional operation step and an intensive review and authorization step.

Using the new process, the company found that it uses the more time-consuming, second path approximately 5 per cent of the time. The other 95 per cent of the time, applications are processed immediately. The resultant cycle time savings are huge.

What's great about using decision points is that we eliminate exceptions. We don't have to treat everything as an exception any longer. Exceptions now become just an alternative process path. Admittedly, these alternative path are often more time consuming. However, a more cautious approach is sometime necessary. In other cases, however, the process is short and simple.

When dealing with exceptions, use decision points and alternate paths. Decision points allow us to process most typical cases in an efficient fashion, and they allow us to identify and treat real exceptions differently. Principle 5 is a good one to remember, especially if your process deals with potentially high-risk situations.

Principle 6: Think parallel, not linear. Most of us think linear. We design processes the same way; in a linear fashion. First you complete step 1, then step 2, then step 3, and so on. Our processes resemble long linear chains, as illustrated in this diagram:

○ → ▷ ○ → ○ → □ → ○ → ▷ ○ →

The problem with linear processes is that they often have lengthy cycle times. Everything must wait for the completion of a previous step before the next step can begin.

One way to improve process efficiency is to think parallel—not linear—

by using convergent and divergent processes whenever possible. For example, the preceding long linear process can be reengineered to look like this:

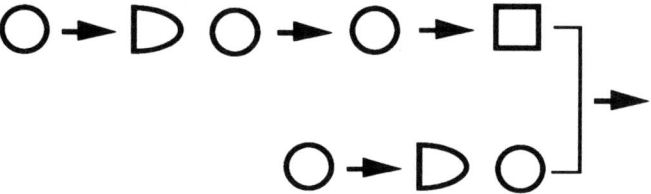

In this example, two parallel processes occur simultaneously. They then converge into a linear process only when it's really needed, but not before. By using parallel, convergent, and divergent processes, we can significantly reduce cycle times.

So think parallel, not linear. Whenever you see a typical process or project schedule that looks like this:

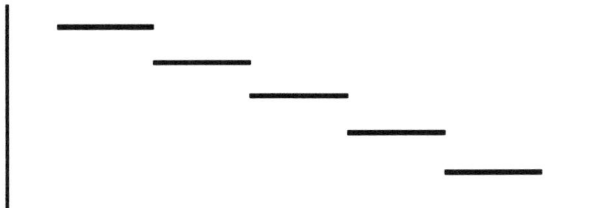

Ask yourself why it can't look like the following process instead:

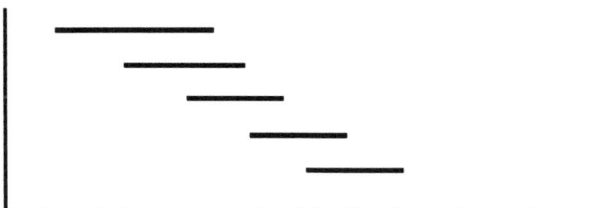

You should also question why some tasks, if not most, can't be accomplished in parallel, and why cycle times can't be significantly reduced.

Principle 6 is all about changing linear processes to parallel processes whenever possible. Parallel is good. When attempting to reengineer any process, always keep parallel processes in mind.

Principle 7: Collect and handle data once at its source. Our jobs often involve collecting and handling information. This is all part of doing business in the Information Age. Unfortunately, we're not very efficient or effective at processing information.

We often collect the same information numerous times. We've all filled out a large stack of forms that repeatedly requested the same information, or completed an administrative or application process that entailed giving the same information to different people. Collecting the same information twice in any process is like rework. We're unnecessarily repeating an operation step:

So, whenever possible, collect needed information only once. Collecting information once is work. Collecting the same information more than once, however, is waste.

Another common problem with processing information occurs when we physically handle the same information twice. For example, we often collect information using pen, paper, and a clipboard, and subsequently enter the information into a computer. In this example, entering information into a computer is similar to rework, because we've already collected it:

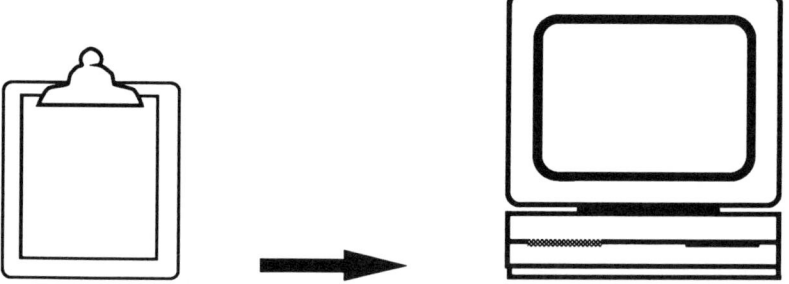

A process also becomes more error prone when we handle information twice. For example, when we collect information in one form (e.g., pen and paper) and then reenter it a second time, we are likely to make a transposition error. A transposition error involves switching numbers or letters. For example, we might use pen and paper to record air pressure as 285 psi, then enter this data into a computer as 825 psi. That's a transposition error. Entering data a second time has a fairly high probability of causing a transposition error, approximately one in every thousand entries.

So, entering the same data twice has two associated problems:

- It's not very efficient.
- It's not very effective.

That is, it's both time consuming and prone to error. The solution? With the introduction of hand-held computers, it has become possible to collect data once at its source. Then we can electronically upload the collected data to a larger computer. Using a small, hand-held computer this way, it becomes a data source entry device, or DSED. This DSED configuration looks like this:

Process Improvement Principles | 99

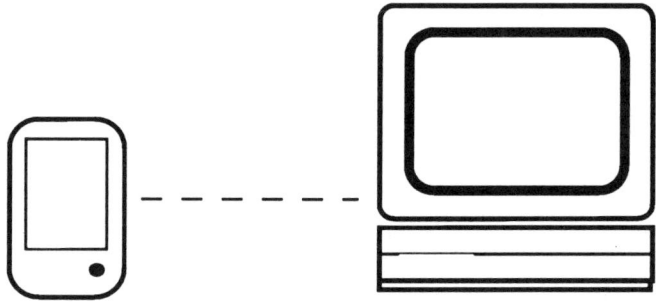

A DSED can minimize the time associated with transforming data from one form to another. It also eliminates the problem of transposition errors because the data is now transferred electronically. Once again, we've used technology—in this case, a DSED—to improve a process.

Whenever possible, collect and handle information only once. Remember that the information should be handled at its source. That's what principle 7 is all about. Following principle 7 not only saves time, it also improves the accuracy of the collected information.

Principle 8: Use technology to improve processes. Some people love technology. They think it can solve everything that ails us. Other people hate it. They view it as a problem, not a solution. The real truth is probably somewhere in between.

Companies frequently buy high-tech equipment simply because it's the thing to do. Everyone else is doing it, so they believe they have to do it as well. They don't want to be left behind. Unfortunately, such companies typically buy all of this high-tech equipment without first thinking about how they will even use it.

Companies also commonly let technology drive the process. This is wrong. The process should drive the technology. You should use the technology to improve the process. Don't build processes around technology.

We can improve our use of technology by viewing it as a means of eliminating or minimizing waste. Try to use it as waste elimination and minimization devices (see Figure 6.7). When we start thinking of high technology in these

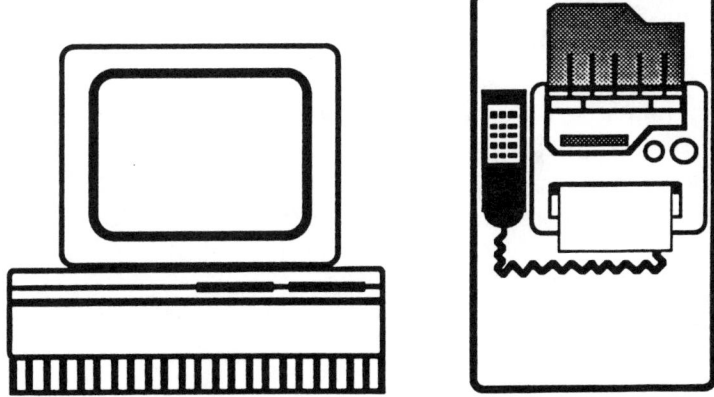

Figure 6.7 Waste elimination and minimization devices.

terms, all kinds of possibilities begin to emerge. When we stop viewing them as expensive, high-tech gadgets, computers, faxes, cellular phones, and other devices take on whole new process functions.

Throughout this book, we've seen numerous examples of using technology to improve process effectiveness, reliability, and efficiency. Think technology, but think of it as a waste eliminator or minimizer: a waste buster! Technology is not just a fancy, expensive, and desperately needed gadget. Technology can help us do things better, faster, and cheaper, but only if we let it. That's what principle 8 is all about.

Principle 9: Let customers assist in the process. When reengineering a process, think of ways to let the customer do some of the work. An Automatic Teller Machine (ATM) is a good example of this principle. ATMs allow customers to start and control the getting-money process. ATMs provide better customer service, and they improve process efficiency and effectiveness. In this instance, the ATM is a customer-activated process control device, or CAPCD.

Customer involvement and CAPCDs are important, but often overlooked process improvement ideas. We mistakenly believe that good service means that we have to do all of the work for the customer. This is not true. Whenever possible, let the customer do some of the work. It increases process efficiency, and makes for happier customers. And happy customers are what we want.

One organization in a large metropolitan city used this idea to improve customer service. The organization is in the business of distributing information to city residents and businesses. To obtain information using the organization's old process, customers had to travel downtown. Those trips typically entailed fighting traffic, finding a parking space, getting a parking ticket, getting upset, and other aggravations. Finally reaching the right place, the customer would fill out a special request form and leave it with a clerk. At some later date, another clerk would search through a massive set of paper files. Finding the requested information the clerk would make a photocopy. Finally, the copy was sent to the customer by yet another clerk. If the customer was lucky, the information would arrive in the mail approximately two to three weeks after it was requested.

With this process, errors were common. When the information finally arrived, it often wasn't what the customer had requested because the customer failed to fill out the requisition form exactly right. When this happened, the customer would have to start the whole process over again: make a trip downtown, fight traffic, find parking space, get parking ticket, be upset, fill out another form, be upset some more, wait another two to three weeks, and hope to get the right information. If not, the customer would get really upset, call the organization, and express what might be euphemistically called a strong opinion.

Sometimes, a single request could take as much as six to nine weeks. By that time, the information often was not needed. Time had run out. Obviously, this was not a very efficient or effective process. This process didn't give customers what they wanted—accurate and timely information.

An analysis of the process revealed numerous transportation, delay, and rework steps, most of which were completely unnecessary. The diagnosis was that radical process reengineering was required. Heeding this advice, management created a new process.

In the new process, the information is stored on optical storage disks in a centralized computer system. The centralized system is connected to a series of satellite computer stations. The newly designed system looks like this:

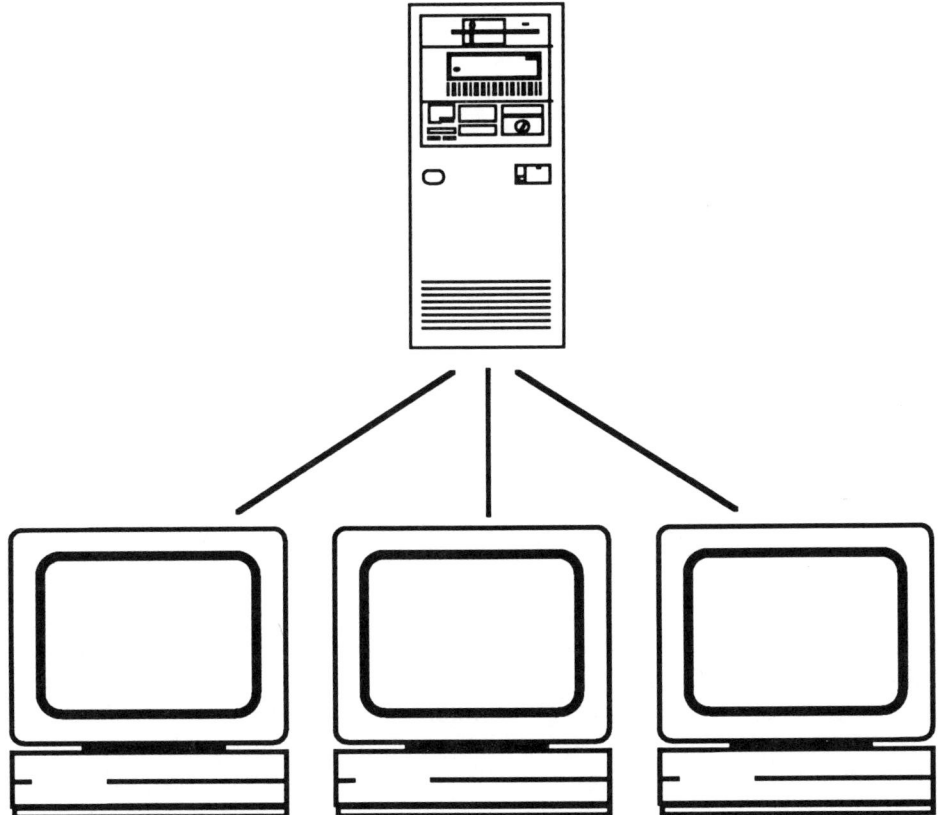

The satellite computer stations were installed at easily accessible sites throughout town. To retrieve information, customers only need to travel to satellite stations near their homes or offices. With a few keystrokes on a computer, they can get the information they want. When certain that they have what they want, they simply press a button for a printed copy.

To a technical person, the new process probably looks like nothing more than a bunch of networked computers. That's true. But as process reengineers, we should view it differently. We should see it as a CAPCD—a customer-activated process control device—a device that lets the customer activate and control the process. The new process provides customers exactly what they want—accurate and timely information—when they want it.

Cycle times used to be between two and nine weeks. Now it's measured in minutes. Information accuracy is also guaranteed. Repeated trips downtown are no longer needed because someone didn't get exactly what they needed the first time. The new process lets customers inspect retrieved information instantly. If it's not right, additional or different information is only a few buttons away.

Whenever possible, get customers directly involved in the process. Let them start it. Let them control it. Let them do some or most of the work. Also, use technology to let them do it. Use technology as a CAPCD. That's what principle 9 is all about; getting the customer directly involved in the process.

Summary

There are countless ways to improve processes and make them better, faster, and cheaper. However, when we examine any process reengineering effort, the basic philosophy is always the same: Eliminate or minimize waste.

Nine principles to follow when reengineering any process are:

1. Eliminate waste.
2. Minimize waste.
3. Simplify everything.
4. Combine process steps whenever possible.
5. Design processes with alternative paths.
6. Think parallel, not linear.
7. Collect data once at its source.
8. Use technology to improve processes.
9. Let customers assist in the process.

If followed, each principle can significantly improve any process, whether that process involves making a product, providing a service, or completing a task.

Principle 8, Use technology to improve processes, is especially relevant in today's high-tech world. Companies often spend fortunes on high-tech equipment, only to be disappointed by subsequent results. Much of the problem stems from failing to view technology as a process waste eliminator or minimizer. We need to start thinking of technology in terms of waste and delay minimization devices, or waste busters! These devices can compress cycle times, reduce process costs, and improve process effectiveness and reliability.

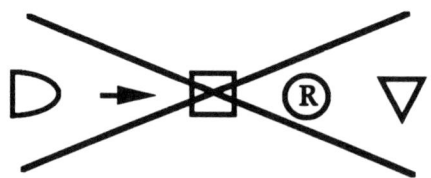

SEVEN

Case Studies

Let's practice and apply what we've learned. This chapter presents five generic case studies. They cover diverse industries and businesses. They also pose a number of different and unique problems. Some of the case studies ask you to complete various steps of the seven-step PI method. Others ask only for your expert opinion.

Case study 1 involves reengineering a delivery system. It asks you to complete the seven-step PI method. Remember, those steps are:

1. Defining process boundaries.
2. Observing process steps.
3. Collecting process-related metrics.
4. Analyzing collected data.
5. Identifying improvement areas.
6. Developing improvements.
7. Implementing and monitoring improvements.

Case study 2 describes a hospital's attempt to reengineer its various administrative processes. You are asked to evaluate the effectiveness of their reengineering process. What would you do differently?

Case study 3 describes an increasingly bothersome problem—ensuring data quality. The case study offers one company's solution to this problem, and asks whether you agree with the solution. If not, how would you do it differently?

In process reengineering, we are usually interested in making huge improvements. We try to cut hours and days from cycle times and save megabucks. Case study 4 is different. It asks you to cut seconds and minutes from an inspection process. You will use the seven-step PI method to micro-reengineer the process.

Case study 5 deals with a bank's process for approving mortgages. You are asked to evaluate its effectiveness and then make some improvement suggestions.

When reading each case study, keep in mind the nine basic process reengineering principles:

1. Eliminate waste.
2. Minimize waste.
3. Simplify everything.
4. Combine process steps whenever possible.
5. Design processes with alternative paths.
6. Think parallel, not linear.
7. Collect data once at its source.
8. Use technology to improve processes.
9. Let customers assist in the process.

Answer the questions posed at the end of each case study. Remember, there is never just one correct answer in process reengineering. Try to achieve the best possible improvement. Your improvement method might be different from someone else's, but that's fine.

Case Study 1

Remember the company that was having trouble with its requisition process? The company took forever to order anything. Then it took even longer to actually get the stuff delivered. This is definitely an inefficient process.

We subdivided the requisition process into three subprocesses:

- Requisition form completion and authorization (req for short).
- Ordering.
- Receiving and delivery.

In Chapters 4 and 5, we worked on the req subprocess. Now let's improve the receiving-and-delivery subprocess.

The company has a large manufacturing complex that is spread out over a large area. You're assigned to analyze and improve the receiving-and-delivery subprocess. Your specific goal is to shorten process cycle time. The subprocess begins with receiving goods on the warehouse loading dock. It ends with the goods being delivered to the correct location.

Using travelers and direct observation, you describe the various process steps. You also record times for each process step. You then average these times. The various steps and averaged times are:

1. Received goods temporarily sit on loading dock (120 minutes).
2. Goods are visually inspected for damage (3 minutes).
3. Goods are carried to the warehouse (10 minutes).
4. Goods are stored in the warehouse (1,440 minutes).
5. Goods are removed from the warehouse and carried to the loading dock (10 minutes).
6. Goods sit on the loading dock awaiting loading (60 minutes).
7. Goods are carried to a truck (10 minutes).
8. Goods are trucked to a satellite storage area (20 minutes).

9. Goods are carried to a satellite storage area (10 minutes).
10. Goods are stored in a satellite storage area (320 minutes).
11. Goods are inspected for damage (2 minutes).
12. Goods are carried to a truck (10 minutes).
13. Goods are trucked to the required location (15 minutes).
14. Goods are carried to the required location (10 minutes).

Using the seven-step PI method starting with Step 2, improve the receiving and delivery process.

Step 2. Observe process steps. Using the process description on the following page, complete the appropriate columns of the process analysis worksheet.

#	Step	Flow	Min	Chart Symbol ○	→	▷	□	▽	®

Step 3. Collect process-related data. Using the process analysis worksheet on the preceding page, complete the metric column.

Step 4. Analyze collected data. Complete the data summary chart and the bar graph.

Step		Steps	Minutes
Operation	○		
Transportation	➤		
Delay	⊳		
Inspection	☐		
Storage	▽		
Rework	Ⓡ		
Total			

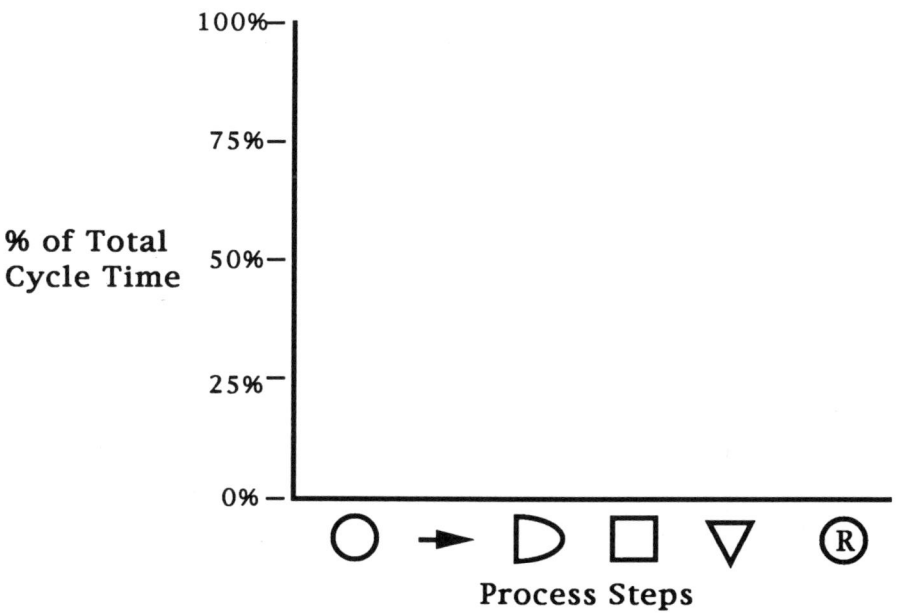

Step 5. Identify improvement areas. Identify and prioritize potential improvement areas.

Step 6. Develop improvements. Develop an improvement strategy and complete the Before-After chart.

Step	Before		After	
	Steps	Minutes	Steps	Minutes
Operation ○				
Transportation ▶				
Delay ▷				
Inspection □				
Storage ▽				
Rework ⓡ				
Total				

Step 7. Implement and monitor improvements. How would you implement the developed improvement? How would you monitor its performance?

Case Study 2

As the Director of Administration for a large hospital complex, you receive some disturbing news. A recent auditor's report states that 28 percent of all hospital costs are related to administrative costs. You are determined to lower this figure. You've read some magazine and newspaper articles about process reengineering. You decide to try it and see if it works.

You call a special off-site meeting. The meeting is held at a luxury hotel. You invite only senior-level managers.

At the meeting, you present your concerns. You then state the purpose of the meeting. It's to reengineer the various administrative processes. Your first task is to brainstorm potential problems. Once a list of problems is generated, you have the assembled group prioritize them.

You then attempt to develop some solutions. You've also brought a number of high-level process flowcharts with you. You tape these to the walls. Using the flowcharts, you discuss each identified problem.

One suggested solution is a reorganization. The group likes that idea. Instead of 12 major groups, you reorganize into 10. Over the next four hours, you hammer out the details of the reorganization. Going back to work the next day, you announce the reorganization plan.

Sitting in your office, you reflect on your first process reengineering efforts. You're quite pleased. Perhaps this stuff really does work!

Evaluate this scenario.

- Is it acceptable?
- Are there any major flaws? If so, what are they?
- How would you conduct this process reengineering effort differently?

Case Study 3

An environmental company specializes in developing computer models. The models display the direction of ground water flow. They are used to predict the movement of pollutants. The company's major customers are state and federal agencies.

The development of the computer models is a fairly complex process. First, numerous water wells are drilled in an area. Then probes are lowered into each well at various depths. From instruments attached to the probes, a number of recordings are made. This is done by field technicians who record the data on paper forms. The data consists mostly of long lists of numbers.

Once back in the office, the numbers are entered into a computer by a data entry clerk. The clerk typically enters hundreds of numbers at a time. The entered data is then used to develop the computer models.

Recently, the company has experienced numerous problems with data quality. Numerous data entry errors have resulted in false models being generated. When this happens, someone must carefully review the entered data. When the incorrect numbers are identified, they are reentered and another computer model is generated. This rework process often must be repeated more than once.

Because it takes a long time to generate the models, such errors add considerable cost and time. However, these additional costs cannot be passed on to the customer. Prices for the computer models come from fixed bids. The company must eat all rework costs.

Alarmingly, rework costs have recently skyrocketed. On the last two jobs, such additional costs eliminated all profits. The company decides to fix the problem. They hire a consultant who is an expert in data quality.

The consultant makes a series of random inspections. First, the consultant checks the original numbers recorded by the field technicians. They all seem correct. So far, so good. Next, the consultant examines the data entered by the data entry clerks. Numerous transposition errors are identified. Some of the errors are huge. For example, one error changed 1,927 to 9,127; another changed 1,898 to 8,198.

The consultant proposes some process changes, including adding an inspection step after the computer data entry step. The consultant suggests that someone other than the data entry clerk should perform this inspection. Because there are hundreds of numbers for each model, the additional inspection step will take some time. However, the consultant can think of no other way to prevent the data entry errors.

The proposed process looks like this:

1. Field technicians record data on paper forms.
2. The data is then entered into a computer by data entry clerks.
3. A printout of the data base is made and a second employee cross-checks the data and the original forms.
4. Any necessary corrections are made.
5. The computer model is generated.

Do the following:

- Develop a simple process flow diagram of the consultant's suggestions.

- Do you agree with the consultant's improvement strategy?

- If not, why?

- Will the consultant's improvement strategy prevent errors from occurring? If not, why?

- Is the consultant's improvement strategy cost effective? If not, why?

- Does it reduce cycle time? If not, why?

- Would you do anything different? What?

- What does your proposed new process look like? Draw a process flow diagram to illustrate the steps.

Case Study 4

A company specializes in storing highly toxic chemicals. Some of the chemicals are so dangerous that they are kept in large, air-tight vaults. To reduce the risk of explosion, all oxygen is pumped from the vaults.

The chemicals are stored in metal containers. The containers are kept in long storage racks. The racks are located along the sides of the vault. Approximately 1,000 containers are stored in each vault.

Federal laws require that each container is visually inspected once a month. Failure to comply with this requirement can result in expensive fines and loss of storage permits. The inspection involves:

- Cross-checking the labels and identification numbers with printed records.
- Visually inspecting for any leakage.

Because of the lack of oxygen in the vaults, inspection personnel must wear a breathing apparatus. Air supply is approximately 60 minutes. However, for safety reasons, personnel are allowed to be in the vaults for only 45 minutes at a time. Two people are in the vaults at any time. Each inspector works independently.

The multiple entries required by the inspections are very costly and potentially dangerous. You are asked to analyze the inspection process. Specifically, you are asked if more inspections can be completed in the allotted 45 minutes.

You are given a diagram of the vault. You note that each container is numbered. Containers are also stored in numerical order. That is, container 104657 is next to container 104658, which is located next to container 104659, which is next to container 104660, and so on. In this case, the first three digits—104—indicate the vault number. The last three digits indicate the container number.

Once personnel are in the vault, the inspection process consists of:

1. Walking to the first container.
2. Searching for the correct container ID number in the index of the records manual.
3. Turning to the appropriate page.
4. Cross-checking this information with the container label.
5. Visually inspecting the container.
6. Moving to the next container.
7. Repeating steps 2–5.
8. Moving to the next container.
9. Repeating steps 2–5.

This process is repeated until 45 minutes have elapsed. At that time, inspection personnel must exit the vault.

You accompany inspection personnel into the vault. You complete a process analysis worksheet. Part of it is shown on the next page. Note that time is recorded in seconds (Sec). On average, approximately 12 to 14 containers are inspected by each person during a 45 minute inspection.

A copy of an index page from the records manual used during the inspections is shown on the following page.

#	Step	Flow	Sec	Chart Symbols ○ → D □ ▽ ®
1	Walk to first container.	→	60	
2	Search for container ID # in index.	D	120	
3	Search for and find right page.	D	5	
4	Cross-check information.	□	20	
5	Visually inspect container.	□	30	
6	Move to next container.	→	5	

Container ID # and Page Index

104001–p. 6   104660–p. 666
106235–p. 40   105222–p. 228
102676–p. 82   103586–p. 592
104911–p. 917   101354–p. 360
104659–p. 666   104173–p. 179
101118–p. 124   106009–p. 15
103773–p. 779   102428–p. 434

Numbering Continues In This Manner

Conduct a microanalysis of steps 2–5. Recall, the steps are:

2. Search for the container ID number in the index.
3. Turn to the appropriate page.
4. Cross-check the information.
5. Visually inspect the container.

Complete steps 4–7 of the seven-step PI method. Use only this mini-sequence (i.e., steps 2–5) for your analysis. When finished, determine how many more inspections can be completed during each 45-minute vault entry.

Step 4. Analyze collected data. Complete the data summary chart and the bar graph.

Step		Steps	Minutes
Operation	○		
Transportation	➤		
Delay	D		
Inspection	□		
Storage	▽		
Rework	Ⓡ		
Total			

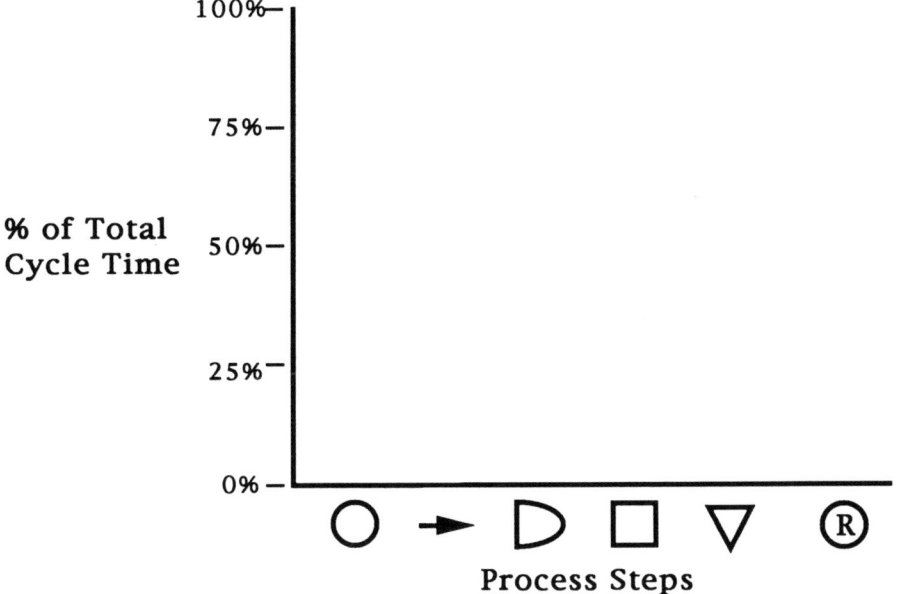

Step 5. Identify improvement areas. Identify and prioritize potential improvement areas.

Step 6. Develop improvements. Develop an improvement strategy and complete the Before-After chart.

	Before		After	
Step	Steps	Minutes	Steps	Minutes
Operation ○				
Transportation ▶				
Delay ᗡ				
Inspection □				
Storage ▽				
Rework Ⓡ				
Total				

Step 7. Implement and monitor improvements. How would you implement the developed improvement? How would you monitor its performance?

On the basis of your improvement method, how many more inspections can be completed during a 45-minute vault entry? Assume that you have only 40 minutes to actually conduct the inspections.

Case Study 5

You have just changed jobs and moved to a new city. You make a down payment on a new home and go to the bank to apply for a mortgage. The person you deal with at the bank seems very efficient. You are surprised, however, when you are told that it will take approximately 6 to 8 weeks to process your loan application. You ask why it takes so long.

Trying to appease you, the loan officer shows you a lengthy process flow diagram. You listen to a lengthy description of the linear steps. There are numerous steps.

"Why so many steps," you ask.

"We simply can't be too careful," the loan officer replies. "Some people default on their loans. That costs us lots of money."

"But I've never defaulted on anything in my life," you reply. "I have excellent credit."

"Oh I'm sure that's true," the loan officer remarks. "But at our bank, we treat everyone exactly the same. Good credit, bad credit, or no credit, all mortgage applications are processed the same. We're very proud of that fact."

How would you evaluate this encounter? Do you see anything that's begging for improvement? If asked, how would you reengineer the mortgage application process? What specific steps would you follow?

Summary

The five case studies represent just the tip of the iceberg of processes needing reengineering. Wherever we look, there's a process in need of significant improvement and waste that needs to be eliminated.

WASTE
IS
EVERYWHERE

Some Final Comments

That's it. We've reached the end. But before closing, let's quickly review some of the key points we've made in *The Process Reengineering Workbook*. Let's also try to dispel some common myths about process reengineering.

Key Points

1. We have to start rethinking and reengineering the way we do business. We need to focus on the *what*, not the *who*. We need to reengineer the *what*—that is, our work processes. We need to learn how to work smarter, not harder. We need to make our business processes better, faster, and cheaper.

2. The time we spend on the job can be divided into two components: work and waste. Work occurs whenever an activity is moving a process forward or adding value to an output. Waste represents all non-value adding activities. Waste includes wasted effort, time, material, motion, costs, and so on. Waste does not add value or move a process forward. Instead, waste adds only delay and cost. Process reengineering is really all about eliminating excessive waste from the workplace.

3. Work efficiency is a mathematical expression of the amount of work—as opposed to waste—in a process. Work efficiency is expressed as:

$$\frac{Work}{Work + Waste} \times 100\%$$

The ideal work efficiency for any process is 100 percent. The closer we get to reaching that ideal number, the better the process.

4. As illustrated in Figure 8.1 process reengineering can result in:

- More work being accomplished in the same amount of time.
- The same amount of work being accomplished in much less time.

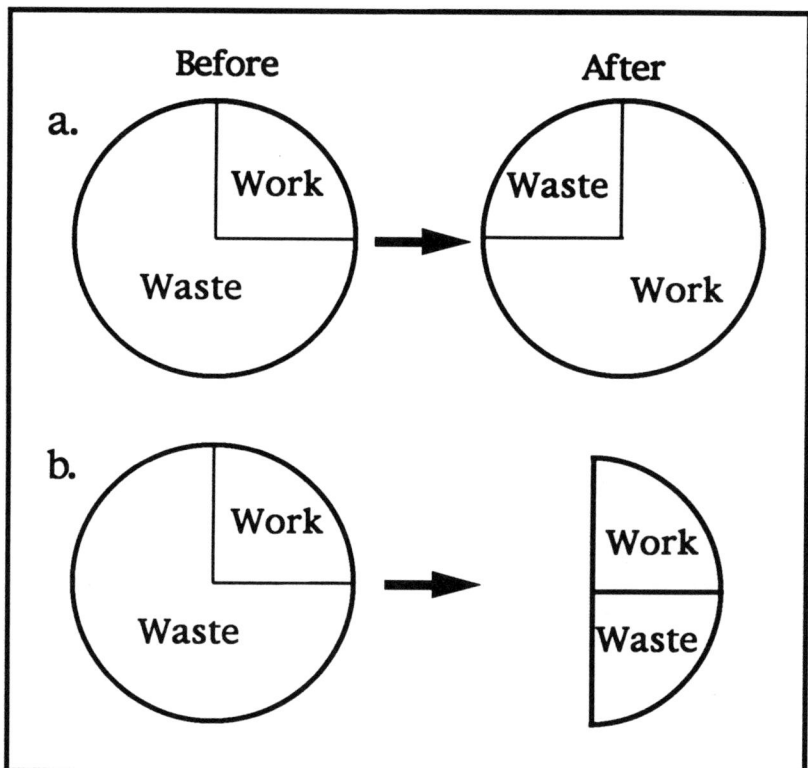

Figure 8.1 Through process reengineering, more work can be done in the same amount of time (a) or the same amount of work can be done in much less time (b).

5. Almost anything can be viewed as a process. A process is the blending and transformation of a specific set of inputs into a more valuable set of outputs. Outputs include:

- Producing a product.
- Providing a service.
- Completing a task.

Inputs can include:

- People.
- Materials.
- Equipment.
- Information.
- Procedures.
- Policies.
- Time.
- Money.

The goal of any process is to transform inputs into outputs as effectively, reliably, efficiently, and cheaply as possible.

6. Outputs go to customers. Customers can be either internal or external. Whether they are internal or external, customers are the most important part of any process.

7. Suppliers provide some of our inputs. Controlling the quality of our inputs is as important as controlling the quality of our outputs.

8. A process model can be created to illustrate the transformation of inputs into outputs. Customers receive outputs. To satisfy customers, we must continually get feedback about our outputs. Suppliers provide some inputs.

A Process Model

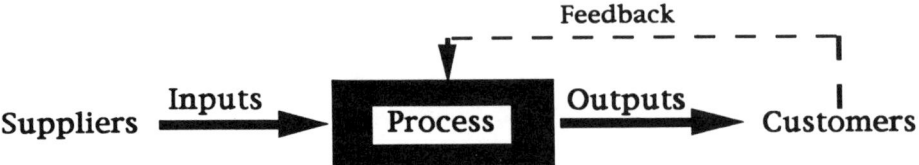

9. Most companies are organized along departmental or functionl lines. As shown in the following diagram, individual departments resemble a bunch of separate smokestacks. Nothing is connected. Processes, however, are horizontal. They're like long pipelines. In a process, everything is connected.

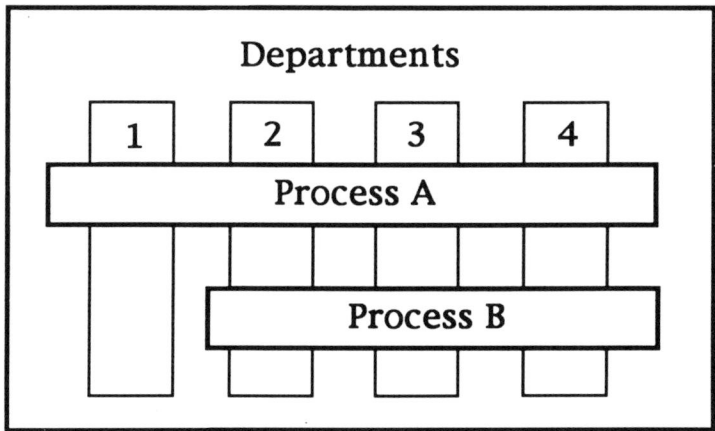

This difference between processes and organizations creates many problems. It spawns turf battles, poor communication, and lousy coordination. To overcome these problems, some companies are beginning to organize along process lines. They are starting to manage their organizations cross-functionally.

10. Any process contains six basic process steps:

Step	Symbol	Description
Operation	◯	Any value-adding step. Directly moves a process forward.
Transportation	➤	Any action that moves information or objects, including people.
Delay (Unscheduled)	D	Unscheduled delay of materials, parts, or products. Any human waiting time.
Inspection	☐	Includes quality and quantity inspections, reviews, and authorizations.
Storage (Scheduled Delay)	▽	Scheduled delay of materials, parts, or products.
Rework	ⓡ	Any unnecessary, repeated operational step.

We can also combine steps in a process. Some typical combinations include:

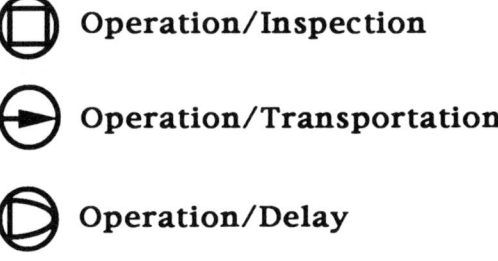

11. The six process steps can be arranged in five basic process sequences. These sequences are:

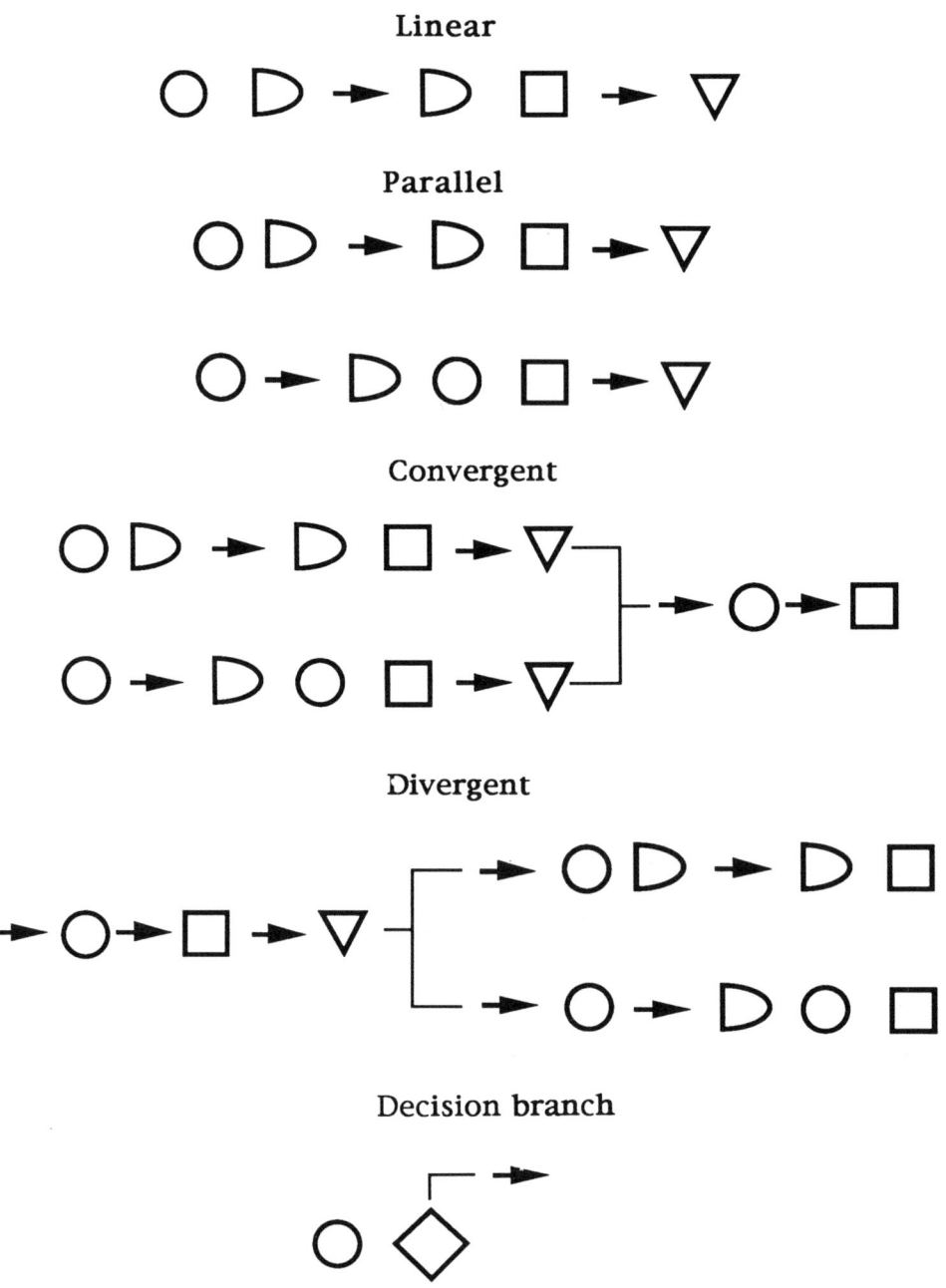

12. Only operation steps directly add value and move a process forward. The other five steps add cost and delay.

Step	Symbol	Work	Waste
Operation	○	✗	
Inspection	□		✗
Delay (Unscheduled)	D		✗
Transportation	→		✗
Storage (Scheduled Delay)	▽		✗
Rework	ⓡ		✗

Whenever possible, these five steps should be eliminated:

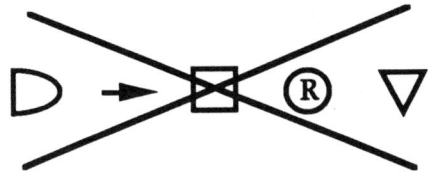

13. To significantly improve a process, we have to first learn something about it. That knowledge can be acquired by conducting a process analysis. A process analysis describes the different types of steps associated with a particular process. It identifies both value-adding (i.e., work) and non-value adding (i.e., waste) process steps.

14. A process analysis also lets us capture quantitative data called metrics. Time, cost, distance, and number of people are all process-related metrics.

15. There are different types of process analyses. Two that we used are:

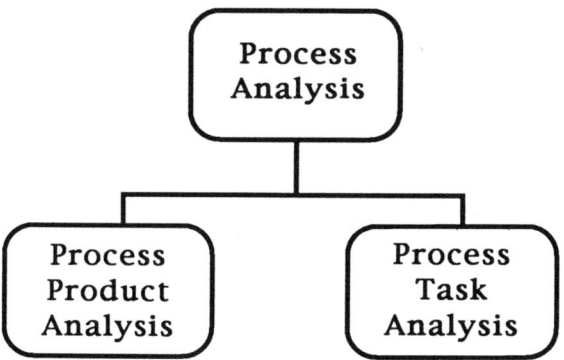

A process task analysis focuses on a human activity. A process product analysis focuses on what is being done to an object.

16. The goal of a process analysis may include:

- Increasing output quality.
- Increasing process efficiency.
- Decreasing process-related costs.
- Making work easier and less fatiguing.
- Making work safer.

17. A process analysis consists of:

- Observing and recording each process step.
- Placing each step in its proper sequence.
- Identifying each type of step.
- Recording all relevant metrics.

18. A process analysis worksheet and a data summary chart are useful tools for conducting a process analysis. Process overhead view diagrams and process flow diagrams are also useful.

19. The seven-step PI method involves:

1. Defining process boundaries.
2. Observing process steps.
3. Collecting process-related metrics.
4. Analyzing collected data.
5. Identifying improvement areas.
6. Developing improvements.
7. Implementing and monitoring improvements.

20. Some basic principles to follow when reengineering a process include:

1. Eliminate waste.
2. Minimize waste.
3. Simplify everything.
4. Combine process steps whenever possible.
5. Design processes with alternative paths.
6. Think parallel, not linear.
7. Collect data once at its source.
8. Us technology to improve processes.
9. Let customers assist in the process.

Some Common Myths

Before closing, it might be helpful to dispel some commonly held myths about process reengineering. These myths include:

Myth 1: *Process engineering is difficult.* Process reengineering doesn't have to be difficult. In fact, it can be fairly simple, especially if you follow a systematic method, such as the seven-step PI method. Just take it one step at a time. Before you know it, you've actually accomplished something. You've eliminated a bunch of waste.

Myth 2: *Programs such as process reengineering, process improvement, Total Quality Management, or whatever you want to call it, always fail.* Sometimes these programs do fail, but not always. Factors that seem to affect success include:

- Management commitment.
- Management's ability to communicate that commitment to employees.
- Management staying power.
- Identifying and solving specific problems—not the world.
- Biting off manageable process chunks.
- Paying attention to team and organizational matters.
- Providing real tools that people can use and apply, not just a nice philosophy.
- Fixing things now, not months or years down the road.
- Individualizing off-the-shelf training programs.
- Focusing on all aspects of business: quality, speed, and cost.
- Listening to customers, talking to suppliers, and fixing processes.
- Focusing on the *what*, not the *who*.

Myth 3: *Analysis isn't all that important.* Most of us hate to analyze anything. We don't think it's important. Besides, analysis doesn't represent action, and management loves action. The only problem is this: How can we fix something if we don't know what's broken? How do we know that we're focusing our efforts on a biggie, not something minor? How can we make fact-based—not opinion-based—decisions without any analysis? Some analysis is needed. What we don't want, however, is to fall into the paralysis-by-analysis trap. Analyze a process, but don't analyze it to death.

Myth 4: *The team and organizational stuff isn't all that important.* Many companies assemble process improvement teams and then conduct some type of process-related training. Then they set the teams free. The results are usually unsatisfactory. Why? Because they didn't provide any team training. Don't forget, the team and organizational stuff is important. Don't overlook it.

Myth 5: *Process reengineering applies only to manufacturing settings.* We often think this stuff applies only to manufacturing settings. This is absolutely untrue. We can improve any process in any setting. Process reengineering is particularly relevant for administrative and service processes. It also applies to knowledge work. When it comes to process reengineering, no process is exempt from becoming better, faster, and cheaper.

Myth 6: *You can improve quality or you can improve speed, but you can't improve both.* This is a common misconception. Speed and quality can, and do, go together. Many companies are proving it on a daily basis. The key to improving both speed and quality is in the process. Successful companies first develop effective processes. Then they start making them efficient. The results? With a little time, they improve both quality and speed.

Myth 7: *Technology is the real solution.* Technology is extremely helpful in process reengineering, but it's not the answer in and of itself. Technology should be designed into processes, not the other way around. It should also be used as a waste elimination and minimization device.

Myth 8: *Process reengineering is an exact science, not an art.* Process reengineering is both a science and an art. The best process reengineering solutions blend technology, techniques, principles, and creativity. You should adapt the techniques and ideas presented in this book to your own work setting. If they work for you, they're a success. So, be creative. Think of alternatives. Think in new ways. That's process reengineering.

Myth 9: *Process reengineering is something new.* Although the term process reengineering is fairly new, the concept isn't. In fact, Frank Gilbreth (1868–1924) would feel right at home with the term. In 1895, he started his own company. His company specialized in speed building—that is, building better, faster, and cheaper than the competition. For example, his bricklayers laid approximately 2,600 bricks a day. The competition could do only 500 a day. The keys to his success include:

- Systematically analyzing processes.
- Reducing wasted motion.
- Eliminating unnecessary process steps.
- Developing and implementing supporting technology.

Although this is almost 100 years old, it certainly sounds like process reengineering doesn't it? So, process reengineering might not be as new as we think. Just ask Frank Gilbreth!

Myth 10: *Details and small things don't really count.* It's often the details and the small things that contain all of the waste. Individually, these things don't add up to much. Collectively, however, they cost companies millions of dollars annually. In addition, almost any process looks good from a high enough level. Only when you start examining it at a more detailed level do you see all of the waste. Like it or not, the details are important.

Final Comment

Most companies have a sobering choice ahead. They must get better, faster, and cheaper, or get eaten up by the competition. Not all companies will survive. Some will perish, but others will survive and prosper. These companies will succeed by focusing on the *what*—their basic core processes. And they'll do it using the *who*—people just like you to continually eliminate waste from the workplace.

Glossary

activity—a grouping of several process steps. An activity is the basic division of a subprocess.

before-after chart—a chart comparing expected gains before and after a new process method is implemented.

combination step—a process step that combines two process steps, such as an operation and an inspection step or an operation and a delay step.

complete switchover—the instantaneous implementation of a new process improvement method.

convergent process—a process containing two or more parallel subprocesses that merge into a single linear process.

core process—what a company does for profit—that is, the product or service it produces that external customers are willing to pay for. Two common core processess are selling a specific product and providing a service.

cross-functional management— organizing companies along processes.

customers—recipients of process outputs. They are the most important part of any process.

cycle time- -the length of time it takes a process to cycle once—that is, the amount of time it takes to transform one set of inputs into a set of outputs.

data summary chart—a chart summarizing relevant process-related metrics.

decision branch—a branching point in a process. The selected process branch depends on the decision selected.

delay step—an unscheduled delay of materials, parts, information, or objects. Delays include any human waiting time.

divergent process—a process that splits from a linear process into two or more parallel subprocesses.

effectiveness—the quality of an output—that is, the effect an output has on a customer.

efficiency—the speed at which a process transforms inputs into outputs.

external customers—customers outside of one's own company. These outsiders buy our products or services.

feedback— information from our customers concerning the effectiveness of our outputs.

functional hierarchy—organizing companies along separate departments or functions.

gradual phase in—the gradual implementation of a new process improvement.

inputs—what goes into a process. Some inputs, such as materials or parts, are transformed into outputs. Inputs can include people, materials, equipment, information, procedures, policies, time, or money.

inspection step—includes quality and quantity inspections, reviews, and authorizations.

internal customers—customers who work in the same company as we do.

linear process—a process containing sequential steps. Step 1 is completed before step 2, then step 2 is completed before step 3, and so on.

metric—quantitative, process-related numerical data.

operation step—any value-adding step that alters a process output—this is a step that directly moves a process forward.

output—what a process produces or what is transformed from a specific set of inputs. Outputs can involve producing a product, providing a service, or completing a task. The product, service, and completed task all are outputs.

parallel process—two or more subprocesses occurring simultaneously.

pilot run—initial testing of a new process improvement before it is fully implemented.

process—the blending and transformation of a specific set of inputs into a more valuable set of outputs.

process analysis—a description of the different types of steps associated with a particular process. A process analysis identifies both value-adding (i.e., work) and non-value adding (i.e., waste) process steps. The purpose of a process analysis is to significantly improve a process.

process analysis worksheet—a form used in collecting process-related data, including type of steps, flow, and relevant metrics.

process flow diagram—a symbolic representation of a process sequence.

process overhead view diagram—a bird's-eye sketch of a process. This process map shows the location of each process step and the sequence of steps.

process product analysis—a process analysis that focuses on what is being done to an object.

process task analysis—a process analysis that focuses on a human activity.

profit—the value of outputs minus the cost of the inputs and the process:

$$\text{Profit} = \text{Output Value} - (\text{Input Costs} + \text{Process Costs})$$

reengineering—the radical redesign of a particular process to achieve dramatic improvements in speed, cost, quality, and service. The goal of reengineering is to eliminate or minimize all process-related waste.

reliability—the consistency of an output. A reliable process produces outputs of the same quality, time after time.

rework—any unnecessary, repeated operational step.

Seven-step PI method—a systematic method of analyzing and improving processes. The method consists of seven basic steps:

- Defining process boundaries.
- Observing process steps.
- Collecting process-related data.
- Analyzing collected data.
- Identifying improvement areas.
- Developing improvements.
- Implementing and monitoring improvements.

step—a fundamental unit of any process. There are six basic process steps: operation, transportation, delay, inspection, storage, and rework.

storage step—any scheduled delay of an object. Objects can include materials, parts, and finished or semi-finished products. However, people are not stored, they are only delayed.

subprocess—a division of a process. A process can contain various subprocesses.

suppliers—people who provide inputs. Suppliers are the source of some of our inputs.

transportation step—any action that moves something. This can include moving objects, information, or people.

waste—all non-value adding process activities. Waste includes wasted effort, time, materials, and motion. Waste adds only delay. It should always be eliminated or at least minimized.

what—a work process.

who—humans in a process.

work—actions that move a process forward or directly add value. Work should always be maximized.

work efficiency—a mathematical expression of how much work versus waste exists in a process. Work efficiency is expressed as:

$$\frac{\text{Work}}{\text{Work} + \text{Waste}} \times 100\%$$

Exercise Solutions

Solutions to the exercises on pages 12, 14, 23, 28, 51 and 52 are provided on the following pages. If you can answer these correctly, then you should have no problem with the case studies in Chapter 7. Also, there are no "right" solutions to the case studies. Be creative. Think of different possibilities.

Page 12

Exercise

Identify each activity by circling either **Work** or **Waste**

Performing any non-value adding activity	Work	**Waste**
Searching for information	Work	**Waste**
Assembling two components	**Work**	Waste
Repeating a step in a process	Work	**Waste**
Transporting materials	Work	**Waste**
Performing any value-adding activity	**Work**	Waste
Inspecting a part for defects	Work	**Waste**
Waiting for a meeting to begin	Work	**Waste**
Reentering data a second time	Work	**Waste**
Walking to a service van for a part	Work	**Waste**
Storing material in a warehouse	Work	**Waste**
Capturing data once at the source	**Work**	Waste
Performing any rework step	Work	**Waste**

Page 14

Exercise

For more practice, calculate the work efficiency for the following example. In the example, you must first determine if the activity is work or waste. Then add up the work and waste time columns and plug the totals into the formula.

Activity	Time	Work	Waste
Repair imaging equipment	90	X	
Walk to service van	12		X
Search for needed information	6		X
Walk back to job	12		X
Repair imaging equipment	75	X	
Walk to service van	12		X
Search for needed information	6		X
Walk back to job	12		X
Repair imaging equipment	15	X	

Total Time: __180__ __60__

Work Efficiency:

$$\frac{180}{180 + 60} \times 100\% = 75\%$$

Page 23

Exercise

Try this example. Two companies, X and Y, offer identical services. Company X charges $40 for their service. Company Y charges $35. Supplies for both companies cost $10. Process costs for Company X are $25. Process costs for Company Y are $15.

- Which company makes the most profit per service call?

    Company X profit = $40 − ($10 + $25) = $5

    Company Y profit = $35 − ($10 + $15) = $10

    Company Y makes the most profit.

- By how much?

    $10 − $5 = $5

    Company Y makes $5 more profit per service call.

- Which company do you think is the most competitive?

    Company Y. It has the highest profitability.

Page 28

Exercise

Check the correct step type.

Description	◯	→	◻ (D)	☐	▽	®
Searching for information.			X			
Assembling two components.	X					
Repeating a step in a process.						X
Moving materials.		X				
Reviewing a report.				X		
Waiting for a meeting to begin.			X			
Reentering data a second time.						X
Walking to a service van.		X				
Faxing information.		X				
Storing material in a warehouse.					X	
Capturing data once at its source.	X					
Performing a QC inspection.				X		
Waiting for a printout.			X			
Authorizing a form request.				X		
Leaving a form in an in basket.			X			
Encountering a scheduled delay.					X	

Page 51

#	Step	Flow	Min	Chart Symbol
				◯ ➡ D ☐ ▽ ®
1	Walk to parts bin.	➡	2	➡
2	Search for legs.	D	1	D
3	Carry legs back to workbench.	➡	2	➡
4	Attach legs.	◯	5	◯
5	Walk to parts bin.	➡	2	➡
6	Search for arms.	D	1	D
7	Carry arms back to workbench.	➡	2	➡
8	Attach arms.	◯	3	◯
9	Walk to parts bin.	➡	2	➡
10	Search for head.	D	1	D
11	Carry head back to workbench.	➡	2	➡
12	Attach head.	◯	2	◯
13	Do quality check.	☐	2	☐
14	Carry assembled widget to bin.	➡	3	➡

Page 52

Data Summary Chart

Step		Steps	Minutes
Operation	○	3	10
Transportation	▶	7	15
Delay	D	3	3
Inspection	□	1	2
Storage	▽		
Rework	ⓡ		
Total		14	30

Page 52

Work Efficiency:

$$\frac{10}{10 + 20} \times 100\% = 33\%$$

Process Cycle Time:

$$10 + 15 + 3 + 2 = 30 \text{ minutes}$$

Page 52

Total Labor Costs:

30 minutes = .5 hours

.5 × $40 (hour labor rate) = $20 per widget assembly

Total Waste Costs:

$$\text{Waste} = 15 + 3 + 2 = 20 \text{ minutes}$$

$$20 \text{ minutes} = .33 \text{ hours}$$

$$.33 \times \$40 = \$13.20$$

Page 52

"How's the widget assembly process doing?"

Not very good. Work efficiency is only 33%. Of a total of $20 labor costs per widget assembly, $13.20 goes for waste. This process obviously needs some reengineering.

Suggested Reading

If you want to learn more about process reengineering, the following books and articles are good sources of information. For those primarily interested in traditional manufacturing settings, I especially recommend the book by Ishiwata. For those interested in a more senior-level management approach to process reengineering, I strongly suggest Hammer and Champy's book. Those wishing to employ a broader range of basic quality improvement tools, I advise consulting Michael R. Kelly's book. History buffs interested in some of the early beginnings of process reengineering may find the book by Gilbreth and Carey or my own article informative.

Blackburn, J. D. (1991). *Time-Based Competition: The Next Battle in American Manufacturing*. Homewood, IL: Business One Irwin.

Gilbreth, F. B., Jr., and Carey, E. G. (1988). *Cheaper by the Dozen*. New York: Bantam Books.

Hammer, M. (1990). "Reengineering Work: Don't Automate, Obliterate." *Harvard Business Review*, July–August, p. 68–73.

Hammer, M., and Champy, J. (1993). *Reengineering the Corporation*. New York: Harper Business.

Harbour, J. L. (1993). "Increasing efficiency: A Process-Oriented Approach." *Performance Improvement Quarterly*, 6(4), p. 92–114.

Imo, M. (1986). *Kaizen: The key to Japan's Competitive Success*. New York: Random House.

Ishiwata, J. (1991). *Productivity Through Process Analysis*. Cambridge: Productivity Press.

Kelly, M. R. (1992). *Everyone's Problem Solving Handbook: Step-by-Step Solutions for Quality Improvement*. White Plains, NY: Quality Resources.

Peters, T. (1992). *Liberation Management*. New York: Alfred A. Knopf.

Robinson, A. (1991). *Continuous Improvement in Operations*. Cambridge: Productivity Press.

Shingo, S. (1990). *The Shingo Production Management System: Improving Process Functions.* Cambridge: Productivity Press.

Stalk, G. Jr. (1988). "Time—The Next Source of Competitive Advantage," *Harvard Business Review*, September–October, p. 41–51.

Index

Activity, 31–32
  defined, 127
Administrative processes,
  efficiency, 47–48, 124
  (*see also* Technology)
Alternative path processes,
  85, 95–96, 102
Analysis. *See* Process
  analysis and
  measurement
Assembling parts, steps in,
  38
Automatic Teller Machine
  (ATM), 100–102

Before-after chart, 68, 75,
  76, 83
  defined, 127
Black box, process, 25–28
Boundaries, defining
  process, 55–56, 57–
  59, 70, 71, 77

CAPCD (customer-
  activated process
  control device), 100–
  102
Case studies, 103–15
Collection of data, 63–65,
  70, 73, 80, 107
  at source, 85, 97–99,
  102

Combination step, 32, 35,
  85, 91–94, 102
  defined, 127
Company organization,
  20–23, 118–19
  complex processes, 91
  efficiency, 47–48
  teams, 56, 123
Complete switchover, 70
  defined, 127
Complex processes, 89–91
Computers, 98–100, 101
Consistency, 24
Convergent process
  sequence, 30, 35, 120
  defined, 127
Core process outputs, 21–
  22
  defined, 127
Cost-benefit analysis, 67
Costs
  complex processes, 89
  decreasing process, 3,
  25
  exercise, 33, 133, 136–
  37
  input-output, 21–22, 24
  as metric, 37, 121
  profit and, 22–23
  waste and, 7, 16, 32–
  33, 35, 44–45
Cross-functional
  management, 21
  defined, 127

Customer-activated process
  control device
  (CAPCD), 100–102
Customers
  defined, 127
  involvement in process
  improvement, 85,
  100–102
  listening to, 25
  as output recipients,
  18–19, 20, 34, 118
Cycle time, 3, 24–25, 39
  CAPCD lessening, 102
  defined, 127
  seven-step PI method,
  56
  simplification and
  shorter, 89

Data
  collection of process-
  related, 11, 63–65, 70,
  73, 80, 107
  collection at source, 85,
  97–99, 102
  as input, 18, 118
  process analysis, 36–37,
  53, 56, 65–66, 70, 74,
  107, 113
  processing errors, 98–
  99
  quantitative, 4, 37, 41,
  48, 54, 56

141

Data summary chart, 41, 43, 46–47, 48, 52, 53, 54, 65–66, 74, 81, 107, 113, 122, 136
  defined, 127
Decision branch
  defined, 127
  process sequence, 30, 35, 120
Decision point and branches, 31, 95–96
  symbol, 31
Defect rates, 89, 90, 93, 98
Delay stop
  as basic process step, 3, 25, 34, 35
  complex processes, 90–91
  defined, 127
  description, 27
  as improvement target, 66
  in process product analysis, 39, 45–46
  in process task analysis, 38
  scheduled (*see* Storage step)
  sequence in process, 29, 38
  symbol, 27, 29, 33
  as waste, 7, 8, 9, 16, 32, 33, 35, 85, 86, 119, 121
Departmental organization, 20–23
Details, myths about, 124–25
Development ideas, 67–69, 70, 74–76, 82–83
Distance, as metric, 37, 121
Divergent process sequence, 30, 31, 35, 120
  defined, 127

Effectiveness, 24
  defined, 127
Efficiency
  administrative process, 47
  decision branches, 31, 95–96
  defined, 127
  as key process characteristic, 15, 24–25
  process analysis, 39
  process engineering for, 15, 16, 47–48, 83
  process improvement, 76
  work, calculation of, 13–14, 16, 43–44, 47, 76, 81, 116, 129, 132, 136
"Eliminate, simplify, and combine," 67
Elimination of waste, 6–16, 23, 36–37, 85–86, 99–100, 102, 125
Equipment, as input, 18, 34, 118
Errors. *See* Defect rate
Exercises
  cost efficiency, 23
  input/output, 20
  process analysis, 49–50
  process step identification, 28
  solutions, 130–37
  work efficiency calculation, 14
  work or waste identification, 12
External customers, 18, 19, 34
  defined, 128

Feedback, defined, 128
Flowchart models, 18, 19, 34, 62–63, 82, 118, 128

Functional hierarchy, 20–23
  defined, 128

"Garbage in, garbage out," 19
Gilbreth, Frank, 124
Glossary, 127–29
Goals, setting large, 56–57
Gradual phase in, 70
  defined, 128

High-tech equipment. *See* Technology
Human activity. *See* People

Identification
  of improvement implementation method, 70
  of improvement targets, 66–67, 70, 74, 82, 107
  of process for improvement, 55–56
  of waste, 11–12, 37, 45 (*see also* Process analysis and measurement)
Implementation, process improvement, 70, 76, 83
Improvement, process. *See* Process improvement
Information. *See* Data
Inputs
  costs, 21–22
  defined, 128
  examples, 18, 34, 118
  processing of, 1, 3, 17, 21–22, 34
  suppliers, 19, 20
Inspection step
  as basic process step, 3, 25, 34

combining steps in, 91–93
defined, 128
description, 27
as improvement target, 3, 25, 34, 66
and process complexity, 90–91
in process product analysis, 39
in process task analysis, 38
representing waste, 3, 25, 85, 86, 121
sequence in process, 29, 38
symbol, 26–27, 29, 33
Internal customers, 18, 19, 34
defined, 128

KISS (keep it simple stupid!), 67, 91

Labor. *See* Work
Linear process sequence, 30, 35, 85, 96–97, 102, 120
defined, 128

Management, cross-functional, 21, 127
Manufacturing, 124
Materials, as input, 18, 34, 118
Measurement, process, 3–4, 36–54 (*see also* Quantitative data)
Metric
defined, 128 (*see also* Quantitative data)
selection of appropriate, 58–59
types, 41, 121
Money, as input, 18, 34, 118 (*see also* Costs)

Monitoring improvements, 70, 73, 76
Myths, about process reengineering, 123

Non-value adding activities. *See* Waste
Numerical data. *See* Quantitative data

Observation
of process steps, 59–63, 70, 71, 77–79, 105–7
techniques, 59, 63
Operation step
adding value, 33, 34, 35, 121
as basic process step, 3, 25, 33, 34, 35, 91
combining steps in, 91, 92–94
defined, 128
description, 27
in process product analysis, 39
in process task analysis, 38
symbol, 26, 27, 29, 33
Organization
process vs. company, 20–23
team work, 56, 123
Outputs
components, 6, 117
costs, 21–22
customers, 18–19, 34, 118
defined, 128
efficiency, 24–25, 39
key process characteristics, 24–25
as process result, 1, 3, 17–18, 20, 21–22, 34
quality improvement, 3, 24
reliability, 24

value, 7–9, 16, 17, 33
work relationship to, 6
Overhead view diagrams, 60, 62, 69, 122
defined, 128

Parallel process sequence, 30, 35, 85, 96–97, 102, 120
defined, 128
People
complex processes and, 91
as input, 18, 34, 118
as metric, 18, 37, 121
observation cautions, 60
process task analysis, 37, 38, 54, 93–94
as who, 129
see also Customers
Phase in, improvement, 70
Physical effort, for work and waste, 8
PI. *See* Process improvement; Seven-step PI method
Pilot run, 70
defined, 128
Policies, as input, 18, 34, 118
Procedures, as input, 18, 34, 118
Process, 17–35
adding value, 7
alternative paths, 85, 95–96, 102
analysis and measurement, 3–4, 36–54
boundaries, 55–56, 57–59, 70, 71, 77
characteristics, 20–25
combined steps, 32, 85, 91–94, 102, 127
company organization vs., 20–23, 118–19
complexity, 89–91

Process (cont.)
  constant improvement, 25
  core, 21
  costs, 3, 23, 25
  customers, 18–19, 20, 25, 34, 118, 127
  cycle time compression, 3
  data collection, 63–65
  defined, 1, 3, 6, 16, 17, 25, 34, 117, 128
  desired characteristics, 24–25
  division of, 21
  efficiency, 13–14, 15, 16
  exercise, 20
  forward movement of, 7, 16, 32
  graphic illustration, 30–32
  identification, 11–12
  improvement (see Process improvement)
  input/output exercise, 20, 132
  non-value adding activities, 3 (see also Waste)
  observation, 59–63
  profits, 22–23
  radical redesign, 2
  reengineering (see Process reengineering)
  sequence, 29–34
  simplification, 89–91
  six basic steps, 3, 25–29, 34, 35, 38, 119
  speed, 24–25
  subprocesses, 21, 31, 129
  symbols, 26–27, 29
  waste components, 6–11, 32–34, 85, 86
Process analysis and measurement, 36–54
  cautions, 58, 60, 63
  components, 39, 48, 122
  data collection, 37–38, 63–65, 70, 74, 80
  data summary charts, 41, 43, 46, 47, 48, 52, 53, 54, 65–66, 74, 80, 107, 113, 122
  defined, 3–4, 36, 53, 121, 128
  examples, 41–48
  exercise, 49–50
  goals, 53, 122
  myth about, 123
  overhead view diagram, 60, 62, 122
  purpose, 37, 58
  in seven-step PI method, 56–84
  significance of, 48
  summary, 53–54
  types, 37–39, 53, 121–22
Process analysis worksheet, 39–41, 42, 46, 51, 52, 53–54, 60–61, 64, 71, 72, 78, 79, 106, 122
  defined, 128
Process black box, 25–28
Process flow diagram, 18, 19, 34, 62–63, 82, 118
  defined, 128
Process improvement (PI), 2–3, 3–4, 25, 28, 33, 36–54
  analysis for (see Process analysis and measurement)
  basic principles, 85–102, 122
  before-after chart, 68, 75, 76, 83
  boundaries, 55–56, 57–59, 70, 71, 77
  case studies, 103–15
  customer involvement, 100–102
  data collection, 63–65, 70, 73, 80
  development ideas, 67–69, 70, 74–76, 82–83
  identifying areas for, 66–67, 70, 74, 82, 107
  implementing and monitoring, 70, 76, 83
  key points, 116–22
  myths, 123–25
  overhead view diagrams, 60, 62, 69, 122, 128
  priorities, 67
  results, 117
  seven-step method, 4, 55–84, 123, 129
  simplification for, 67, 85, 89–91
  step combination, 91–94
  step observation, 59–63, 70, 71, 77–79
  summary, 102
  technology for, 99–100
  waste elimination (see Waste)
Process overhead view diagram, 60, 62, 69, 122
  defined, 128
Process product analysis, 121, 122
  defined, 37, 38, 53, 128
  example, 45–48
  steps, 38–39
Process reengineering
  administrative processes and, 47–48, 124
  analysis and measurement, 3–4, 36–54
  applications, 124
  basic principles, 85–102, 122

as both science and art, 124
case studies, 103–15
defined, 2, 116, 129
goals, 15–16, 56–57
golden rule, 85
historical use of, 124
key points, 116–22
myths, 123–25
reasons for program failure, 55
seven-step PI method for, 4, 55–84, 123
summary, 102
waste elimination, 6–16, 85–86
waste minimization, 87–89
work definition, 6
Process sequence, 29–34
activity, 31–32, 127
analysis, 36–39, 48, 53, 54
basic steps, 3, 25–29, 34, 35, 55, 119, 129, 134
exercise, 134, 135
graphic illustration, 30
improvement from, 85
as improvement target, 66
product analysis, 38–39
simplification, 89–91
step combinations, 32, 35, 85, 91–94, 102, 119–20
step identification exercise, 28
symbols, 29
task analysis, 38, 39
value-adding step, 33
waste-representing steps, 33, 85, 86
Process steps. *See* Process sequence
Process task analysis, 121
defined, 37, 38, 53, 128
example, 41–45
focus, 122
importance for efficiency, 47–48
steps, 38
Process waste. *See* Waste
Product
as output, 1, 6, 17, 117
process analysis, 37, 38–39, 128
Profit
costs and, 22–23
defined, 128
equation, 22

Quality
effectiveness, 24, 127
improvement of output, 3, 24
input-output relationship, 19, 20, 118
myth about, 124
reliability, 24
see also Inspection step
Quantitative data, 4, 41, 48, 54
before-after chart, 68
collection, 56, 63–65
defined, 37, 128
importance of, 71
for improvement prioritization, 67
selection of appropriate, 58–59
types, 37, 121

Radical redesign. *See* Process reengineering
Ratio, work to waste, 13, 16
Reengineering. *See* Process reengineering
Reliability, 24
defined, 129

Rework
as basic process step, 3, 25, 34
defined, 129
description, 27
as improvement target, 3, 25, 34, 66
representing waste, 10, 33, 85, 86, 121
symbol, 27, 29, 33

Satisfaction, customer, 18–19
Scheduled delay. *See* Storage step
Sequence. *See* Process sequence
Service, as output, 1, 6, 17–18, 117
Seven-step Pi method, 4, 55–85, 123
case studies, 103–15
components, 55, 84, 122, 129
data analysis, 65–66, 74, 81
data collection, 63–65, 70, 73, 80
defined, 129
defining boundaries, 55–56, 57–59, 70, 71, 77
examples, 71–83
exercise, 135, 136
identifying improvement areas, 66–67, 74, 82
implementing/ monitoring improvements, 70, 76, 83
improvement development, 67–69, 74–76, 82–83
observation, 59–63, 70, 71, 77–79

Seven-step PI (*cont.*)
  procedure, 55–57
  summary, 70–71
  summary of examples, 83–84
  use of teams, 56
Simplification, 67, 85, 89–91, 94, 102
Speed vs. quality, myth about, 124
Steps, process
  defined, 129
  see also Process sequence; *specific steps*
Steps, process improvement method. *See* Seven–step PI method
Storage step
  as basic process step, 3, 25, 34, 35, 121
  defined, 129
  description, 27
  as improvement target, 66
  in process product analysis, 39
  in process task analysis, 38
  representing waste, 33, 85, 86
  sequence in process, 29
  symbol, 27, 29, 33
Subprocess, 31
  defined, 21, 129
Suppliers, 18, 19, 20, 25, 34, 118
  defined, 129
Switchover, 70, 127
Symbols
  decision point, 31
  process, 26, 27, 29, 33
  process combination, 32
  process product analysis steps, 39
  process task analysis steps, 38

Task analysis. *See* Process task analysis
Task completion, as output, 1, 6, 18, 117
Teams, seven-step PI method, 56, 123
Technology
  myth about, 124
  process performance improvement, 3, 85, 87, 88–89, 98–102
Thinking, linear vs. parallel, 30, 35, 96–97, 102
Time
  delay as waste, 3, 7, 8, 9, 16
  as input, 18, 34, 118
  as metric, 37, 121
  process analysis, 39, 54
Transportation step
  as basic process step, 3, 25, 34, 35
  complex processes, 90–91
  defined, 129
  description, 27
  as improvement target, 66, 74–75, 82
  in process product analysis, 39, 46
  in process task analysis, 38
  representing waste, 33, 85, 86, 121
  sequence in process, 29, 38
  symbol, 26, 27, 29

Unscheduled delay. *See* Delay

Value
  core output, 21–22
  operational steps adding, 33, 34, 35, 121
  output, 7–9, 16, 17, 33
  profit and, 22
Value-adding activities, 7, 32, 53, 121
Videotape, 53

Waiting time. *See* Delay
Waste, 32–34, 115
  components, 6–8
  costs of, 7, 16, 44–45
  defined, 3, 16, 116, 129
  delay as, 7, 8, 9, 16
  elimination, 6–16, 23, 36–37, 85–86, 99–100, 102, 125
  examples, 8–11
  exercise, 20
  identification, 11–12, 37, 45
  minimization, 85, 87, 102
  myths about, 124–25
  process analysis to identify, 45, 53, 121
  process steps representing, 33, 34, 35
  profits and, 23
  rework as, 10, 34
  technology to eliminate/minimize, 124
  work efficiency and, 13–14
Wasted time, 3, 7, 8, 9, 16
What
  defined, 129
  focus on, 48
Who
  defined, 129
  focus on, 48
Work
  defined, 6, 32, 116, 129

exercise, 20, 131
operational step
representing, 33, 34, 35, 53
see also Process
Work efficiency
calculation of, 13–14, 16, 43–44, 47, 76, 81, 116, 129
defined, 129
exercise, 132, 136
process engineering for, 15, 16, 83
Work process. *See* Process

Worksheet, process
analysis, 39–41, 42, 46, 51, 52, 53–54, 60–61, 64, 71, 72, 78, 79, 106, 122
defined, 128